Let's Talk About It

A Healing Journey Through Pain to Peace

DENISE STAJKOWSKI

THE
SELF
PUBLISHING
AGENCY

Denise Stajkowski
Let's Talk About It: A Healing Journey Through Pain to Peace

TSPA The Self Publishing Agency, Inc.
Copyright © 2025 by Denise Stajkowski
First Edition

Softcover ISBN 978-1-954233-50-8
eBook ISBN 978-1-954233-49-2

Book Design | Ashley Russell Designs
Editor | Tara McGuire
Cover Photo and Select Photography | Jessica Terkowski
Publishing Management | TSPA The Self Publishing Agency, Inc.

This book is dedicated, with all the love in my heart, to
Gary, Stephen, and Christopher

If you can't fly then run, if you can't run then walk, if you can't walk then crawl, but whatever you do, you have to keep moving forward.

—Martin Luther King Jr.

CONTENTS

AUTHOR'S NOTE

I wrote this memoir with a heart full of love and forgiveness. The events I share are described through the lens of my own perspective, as accurately as I can remember, and I honor that those involved may view the experiences differently. Where appropriate, I have changed names and identifying characteristics to ensure privacy.

INTRODUCTION

The blustery cold air of a spring afternoon in Philadelphia swirled around the parking lot of Abraham Lincoln High School as I nervously paced beside the Pontiac Lemans my older sister Debbie and I shared. Rehearsing my lines over and over in my head, I broke a sweat under the bright sun that beat down on me like a spotlight.

As my sister approached the car, the knot in my stomach tightened and my chest pumped in a cadence I could hear pounding in my ears.

"What happened?" she screamed, looking at the busted back window of the car and the glass on the ground.

"Some kids were tossing around a rock like it was a football and it flew through the back window," I replied.

"What kids?" she demanded over the last part of my reply, looking around for the hoodlums.

"They ran away when I saw them smash the window. I yelled for them to stop, but they took off." I could feel the squeeze of her interrogation.

"How did the car get over here?" she asked, because the car was not in the same parking spot she parked in when we got to school that morning.

"I moved it back here so I could clean it up."

"Then why is there glass on the ground here?"

"Like I said, I was cleaning off the back seat and some of the glass must have spilled out of the car." The sweat now pouring out of me, I was sure she was beginning to figure out something was wrong with this scenario.

"Do you know who the kids were? Maybe I should go tell the principal," she added as she continued to look around for the culprits.

"No, I never saw them before. Maybe they weren't even from this school." I stood there motionless, preparing to be berated for making up such a stupid story.

"This will probably cost a fortune. Fucking kids. Let's go, I have to go to work." And with that, we were off. I was relieved that she was in a hurry.

When we got home, Debbie quickly changed into the uniform for her waitressing job that was just over the bridge in New Jersey. I tried to clean more of the glass out of the car before she had to leave.

"I'll get one of the guys at work to tape some cardboard in the window," she explained as she climbed into the car. "See ya." I watched her drive away and let out a long sigh of relief, grateful that she hadn't figured out I was lying and kicked my ass.

Debbie and I drove to the high school every day together, sometimes picking up stray friends we saw walking along the way. I was fifteen and only had my learner's permit, so I was not allowed to drive the car unless another licensed driver was with me. That day, I loaded some friends into the car, and we went to McDonald's for lunch. None of us had a license. When we came out of McDonald's, I realized I had locked the keys in the car. We were desperate to make it back to school in time for our next class and started to panic. I grabbed a rock from the grass and broke one of the smallest windows in the car, the back, driver's side window.

When we returned to school, the original parking spot was taken. My friends jumped out and ran to their classes, while I stayed behind. I had already become skilled at hiding the truth, so I sat in the car and came up with a lie, never going back inside to finish the school day.

I got detention for ditching the rest of school that afternoon. Debbie wound up paying for the window to be fixed. I don't remember how much it was, but I do remember her bitching about it costing her most of her tips. Surprised that I got away with smashing the window, I thought back over the holes in my story. *Why would there be glass on the ground where I moved the car?* Thank God she didn't go over to the original parking spot because I forgot to put glass on the ground there.

I didn't confess to Debbie about what I had done until we were both in our forties. By then, I figured I could take her if she wanted to give me the ass kicking I deserved. She laughingly chalked it up to the typical chaos our family was used to.

∞

My family of origin, the family I grew up in, consisted of six members. My mother, Patricia; my stepdad, Lou; my older sister, Debbie; my younger brother, Patrick; my younger sister, Jennifer; and me.

My mom, Pat, was a curvy, full-figured powerhouse at five foot three inches. She was a bleach blonde, green-eyed beauty, smart, funny, but distant and closed off. She kept everyone at arm's length. I remember falling off the top of one of those tall, metal sliding boards at the playground when I was seven and landing on the crown of my head. It felt like my entire body collapsed like an accordion until my feet were on the ground next to my ears. I made it into our apartment with tear-soaked dirt smeared on my face. She looked at me and said, "If you're not bleeding, you'll be fine. Go back out and play." Then she went back to cooking dinner. I shouldn't have been surprised, as Mom often told us, "You can find sympathy between shit and syphilis in the dictionary."

I watched my mother try to be the stereotypical wife: cooking, cleaning, ironing, sewing, and serving my dad. She also always worked outside the home as a bookkeeper, so gradually that perfect little lady of the house disappeared. Her career mostly centered around accounting, except when she managed a restaurant for a few years. Mom ended her career holding a high-ranking corporate position in a bank, which was very impressive for someone with an eleventh-grade education.

My stepdad, Lou, who raised me from the age of three, is who I am referring to when you see the word "Dad" in these pages. He was a tall, dark, handsome tough guy from the streets, with thick black glasses and a big, black mustache. He was a Navy Vietnam Veteran, proud American, and funny but strict. Lou kept an upbeat attitude about life for the most part, except when he was mad. He mainly worked in warehouse jobs, ending his career in a supervisor position.

When I think back, I realize they must have been wrapped up in their own issues most of the time, stressed out, distracted, unavailable. They fought a lot about money and their relationship. Dad wasn't as closed off as Mom, but you had to pick up on his unspoken invitations to interact — meaning you had to wait for the right time to get close (what I like to call green light moments). Then, you could sit on his lap while he told you a joke or story.

My sister Debbie was only eighteen months older but was always so much bigger than me. She was awkwardly tall with brown hair and a bossy attitude. We used to call her Moe, like the guy in The Three Stooges. She seemed much more serious than my brother and I, and she didn't have the patience for our childlike silliness.

My brother Patrick was two years younger than me. A dirty blond, scrawny little wise guy who made me laugh and was my favorite person to be around. I was the closest he came to having a brother.

My youngest sister, Jennifer, was seven years younger and the only child my mom and Lou had together. She had dark brown hair and soft brown eyes, just like my stepdad. I loved having a baby sister. It felt like having a live baby doll to play with.

As a young child, I believed everything I saw, heard, and felt. I believed that all families were like the ones I saw on TV in shows like *Leave It to Beaver, Father Knows Best*, and *The Brady Bunch*. Although the children bickered sometimes, there was always a calm resolution to their problems because their parents took the time to listen to how their kids felt. The parents celebrated every accomplishment and expressed how proud they were of their children. In those shows, I saw parents who cared and families that looked like they loved each other. I wished for the same to be true in my family, but I couldn't figure out if it was. I also believed that neighbors and the outside world were like what I saw on *Mister Rogers' Neighborhood* and *Sesame Street*. I expected everyone I met to be kind, friendly, and safe to be around.

I felt confused by the difference between what I saw on TV and how other kids lived, versus how I was treated in our home. I lived by a long list of rules that were repeated like a playlist on a continuous loop: *kids are to be seen and not heard; don't speak unless you are spoken to; do as you are told; respect your elders; no one wants to hear about your problems because we all have enough of our own; don't air your dirty laundry in public.* I got to a point where I didn't know exactly what I was allowed to say, so I learned to say nothing.

The TV shows gave me the impression that home was supposed to be a safe place. The outside world is hard enough to navigate with bullying, reckless adults, and changing environments, but when you also have to navigate the hardships at home, where are you supposed to find comfort, support, and the assurance that all will be okay — where do you go to feel safe?

I didn't even feel safe in my own skin when I was a child, and a feeling of unrest filled my body each day. I often felt attacked by the kids at school, who teased me because I looked different with my orange hair and freckles, and by my mom, who criticized me for acting more like a boy than a girl. My stomach tightened when I was around others, as if I had to brace myself for a punch in the gut.

At night I would lie awake and imagine I was somebody else. Someone with pretty hair and delicate manners, saying and doing all the right things, causing my mother to beam with pride. "That's my Denise, isn't she sweet," were the words that lulled me to sleep, unconsciously, starting the creation of a character that was easier to love.

∞

In 2018, when I initially began writing this book, the title that seemed to fit was *Done with Crazy*. I had the photograph on the cover taken as a testament to my desire to change. My emotional pain had been running the show for fifty-three years. The cycle of generational dysfunction that I had spent so many years trying to escape and so much energy trying to avoid was still showing up in my life every day. I was angry and wondered why I couldn't figure life out. I could feel that I was beginning a new wave of depression, and I was concerned about my long-term well-being. *Is this going to be the depression I never recover from?* In the past thirty years of my mother's life, I witnessed her excessive prescription drug use to numb the pain of her life's disappointments and her anger toward her parents. I wondered if I was headed for the same outcome. I wanted to take control before I lost it completely.

This is the story of how my false beliefs, outdated programming, and judgmental thoughts kept me stuck in patterns that did not allow me to live my best life. Instead, I focused on everything I had done wrong and labeled myself a bad person undeserving of anything better. The book explores the changes I made in my life, on the inside and the outside, and how I went from hiding my deepest shame to experiencing the happiest time of my life.

My intention for writing this memoir was to go through my own healing process. If the book had been released back in 2018, it would've been a finger-pointing book full of blame. I had a lot of work to do, which began with questioning everything I believed about myself.

Since then, I've gotten divorced, moved several times, held multiple jobs, endured three major surgeries, lived through a global pandemic, lost my dad and my stepdad, reflected on my entire life, found peace, and fallen in love. Now is the right time. I've done the work.

Let's Talk About It comes from a lifetime of not talking about the emotional pain I was feeling. My inability to express my emotions resulted from my family's messages of insignificance. Sharing my process has allowed me to come out of hiding and open up about the trauma I experienced in childhood and carried into adulthood. It's a form of freedom I've never felt before.

I created new goals for my life. *Love, joy, freedom*, and *peace* were my new mantras. I contemplated what those words meant, wrote them down in my journals, on sticky notes placed on my bathroom mirror and my computer at work, and recited them in my head while I meditated. Although I believed they were lofty goals, I was determined to stay focused on what I wanted. Surprisingly, I've reached them all, and I'm the happiest I've ever been. I know now that it is never too late to love your life.

Through the process of writing this book and reliving my past experiences, I learned that if you don't believe in yourself, you'll believe in almost anything else. The words on the front cover were my words. What are your words? If you suffer from emotional pain, know that you are not alone. Healing is possible for everyone.

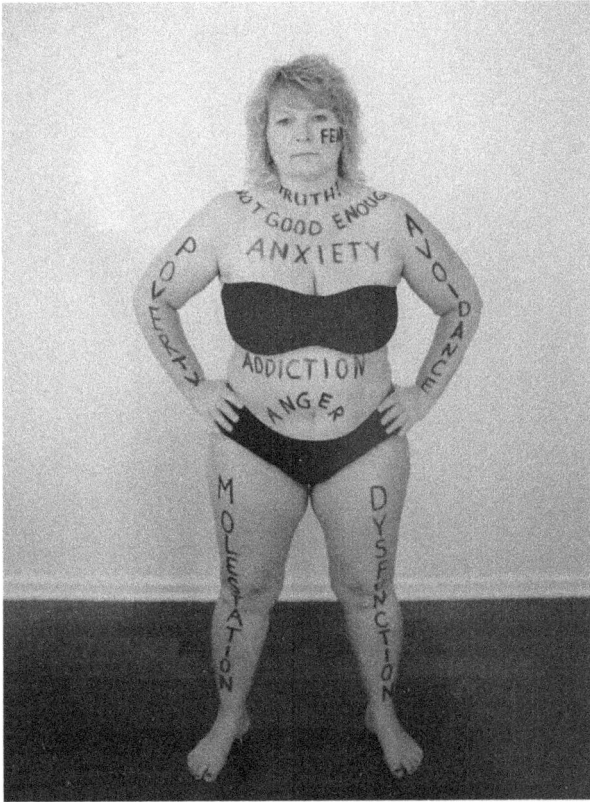

PART ONE
TAKING MY LIFE BACK

Don't get lost in your pain, know that one day your pain will become your cure.

—Rumi

1

THE CATALYST

Each year, in my birth month of April, I take stock of my life, analyzing my level of happiness and where I am on the timeline of my life's achievements — similar to what we all do around New Year's Eve. I'm not sure at what age I flipped from thinking, "I have all the time in the world to figure things out," to "I'm running out of time to figure things out," but I was beginning to feel the noose of time tightening around my life.

In April of 2018, my fifty-third birthday month, I was eating dinner from a tray table in front of the TV, glued to the excessive news coverage of the Bill Cosby sexual assault trial happening just a few miles from my home. I don't normally watch the news but I found myself drawn to this story that felt so personal. My husband Harvey grabbed his plate and joined me in the living room as he had done throughout the past several weeks of the trial. We had both grown up watching Cosby's rise to fame on television and in his family-friendly comedy specials. He was a beloved character and with his clean humor and fatherly image became known as "America's Dad." Now we were watching the famous become infamous.

My stomach churned each day as the reporters recounted the emotional testimonies of the alleged victims and the endless denial of the offender. Those women who came forward to tell their stories seemed unbelievably courageous. Risking their privacy, their reputations, and their futures. Being judged, by some, as harshly as the perpetrator, and having their integrity ridiculed. On this day though, the verdict was to be read, and I had little confidence that justice would be served, given the history of outcomes in other high-profile cases.

Time seemed scattered in my head, jumping from past to present, and I could feel my heart pounding. Painful memories of a time I chose to forget were now in the forefront of my mind. As I anxiously swirled the food around on my plate, I glanced over at my husband for support, recognizing quickly that he didn't know why I felt a link with these women. He looked back with an expression that hinted at understanding but only of our mutual disbelief of Cosby's actions. Neither one of us knew that this was the beginning of the end for our marriage. The air felt thick, and I caught myself holding my breath in anticipation of the decision. I shook with the rush of emotions that flooded my body, and tears filled my eyes when the verdict was finally read. Guilty.

I quickly retreated to the master bathroom to avoid any questions regarding my reaction, keeping my secrets safe. Behind the locked door, years of denial were released in the form of trembling tears. Self-blame had become an involuntary habit that kept me separated from the truth. Although I had put myself in a situation to be preyed upon many years ago, I learned through this trial that I did not deserve to be harmed. With this verdict, I somehow felt vindicated, as if I was the one sitting in that courtroom receiving confirmation that someone believed I had been abused. Believing it myself, I realized for the first time that what happened to me at ten years old was not my fault.

The trial revealed a judgment I'd been carrying around deep inside me for decades. I never thought of myself as a victim but, instead, as a stupid kid who made the wrong choice while trying to help my family. I felt thankful that justice was being served for Cosby's victims. The verdict gave me the strength to face the truth of what had happened to me so long ago. I was molested by someone I trusted. Even though I moved far away from my abuser over forty years ago and buried the pain, I found myself hoping now that somehow justice had caught up to him as well.

EMOTIONAL INVENTORY

I grew increasingly restless in the months that followed the Cosby trial and verdict. After becoming aware that I had blamed myself for the abuse I had suffered, I started to question everything about my life. *If I was wrong about that part of me, what else was I wrong about?* My childhood, sexuality, career, relationships, parenting, and personal habits were all scrutinized. Nothing was beyond dissection.

Self-judgment had always been my companion and did not abandon me as I recollected my life's experiences. Questions swirled around in my head. *Why did my adult life turn out so similarly to a childhood that damaged me? How could I have tried so hard to fix my life and screwed it up anyway? Why did I make so many of the same mistakes I criticized my parents for?*

I'd moved around to over forty different places (twenty before I was eighteen years old), and I'd been a tomboy who roamed through my childhood like a feral cat — afraid of adults. I suffered from anxiety, abandoned my dream of writing and acting for the financial safety of a desk job, searched for validation in promiscuity as a young adult, used food as a way to comfort myself in depression, chased moneymaking opportunities to avoid having to depend on anyone else to support me, had three sons in two different relationships, and walked in some of the same footsteps as my disconnected mother.

The words "I don't belong here" followed me from room to room and day to day like a nagging parent. I was in a marriage that wasn't working, a body full of emotional pain, playing a character that wasn't me. *How did I get here?* My body felt heavy with the answers, and anger welled up in me like I had never allowed it to before. I resented my husband for fighting against my version of acceptable parenting and blamed him for the negative effects I thought his toughness had on the kids. I was tired of being the punchline of his jokes, feeling ridiculed and disrespected. I resented myself for failing to protect my children against dysfunction. Although I worried that the upheaval I'd already put them through caused them emotional harm, I was considering yet another change in my circumstances that would impact their lives.

An inventory of my darkest shame resulted in the picture you see on the cover. A physical embodiment of the parts of me I've worked so hard to keep hidden. The words and phrases were painstakingly chosen to represent the sadness that was stuck in my body and weighing me down. Each one with its own backstory founded in childhood experiences, tender to the touch of reflection, was placed on the parts of my body where I felt it most.

I chose the word *fear* for my cheek, close to where my eyes had seen abuses, my ears heard lies, and the thoughts in my head were telling me I was permanently damaged. As a child, my surroundings felt out of control, and I was helpless to change my circumstances. As an adult, I tried to anticipate what could go wrong, then changed my circumstances, thinking I could outsmart the pain. Out of the fear of recreating the dysfunction of my childhood, my life choices were based more on what I didn't want to happen than what I wanted. The illusion of control was blinding. I could not see that the unwanted dysfunction I focused on only grew.

I heard many different stories from my mother over the years. The word *truth* with a question mark on my throat represents the dishonesty in my family, the inability to express my own truth, and my guilt over not telling the truth at times. Growing up in a household where feelings were buried made it difficult to connect with any kind of internal truth. There was no freedom to express how I felt. Lying was modeled and learned through secret relationships and inaccurate details regarding our family circumstances.

In the photo, I wear the phrase *not good enough* like a necklace. I chased my mother's love, attention, and approval by doing as I was told, excelling in school, obsessing over the way I looked, and becoming the devoted daughter I knew she craved. Even into adulthood, each attempt to impress her made me feel like a child at the playground yelling, "Mommy, look at me!" Her disparaging remarks convinced me that nothing I had done compared to her accomplishments; I was a disappointment. *If I wasn't good enough for my own mother, how could I be good enough for anyone else?* I wore that judgment like a piece of jewelry every day.

Anxiety brought constant feelings of imminent danger. The bold, block letters across my chest cover my lungs that could barely catch a breath during panic attacks, and my heart encased in thick walls that rumbled from the pounding waves of distress, like the hull of a ship in a storm. When I was a kid, that suffocating, nauseous sensation that I was about to die was simply called "worry." I was a highly sensitive child whose insides were in a constant state of turmoil, resulting in long, sleepless nights of being sick. I became hypervigilant, always watching out for trouble with my siblings, my parents, and my surroundings. The feelings that I "have to escape," that I "have to get out," became more frequent and intense as I got older, and I started to avoid any place I couldn't escape from quickly. My mind obsessed over what could go wrong in any situation and how I could get out of it without embarrassing myself. I'd make sure I knew alternate routes to avoid getting caught in traffic jams, I'd pick the end seat of a row at movies and concerts, I'd sit in the closest seat to the door in a business meeting or class, and I'd drive separately wherever I went so that I had control over how I got there and when I could leave. The urge to run was one of the most significant effects of my childhood.

The word *addiction* is on my stomach because I turned to food in times of chaos. I "used" junk food for comfort and to avoid emotions the same way Mom used her pills to escape life's hardships. I consider my mother a prescription drug addict. I watched her ingest pills for every ache, pain, and emotional discomfort and saw how those medications changed her into someone lethargic, uncaring, and numb. When she ran out, she became agitated and unstable. Her erratic behavior caused me to seek out alternative options for my own health issues. Despite our opposing views of the medical community, we both filled our craving for attention with a collection of men, some with their own addictions.

I rejected my anger and buried it deep down in my gut along with a lifetime of other people's anger, so displaying the word *anger* in an arch above my belly felt appropriate. The intensity with which my parents fought frightened me. The way they talked to each other and the hurtful things they said confused me. I heard a lot of blame and name calling in a tone that sounded hateful. *Is this how you love somebody?* My aversion to anger kept me from standing up for myself, which made me feel like a coward at times. My body has a visceral reaction to the slamming of doors, yelling, and any kind of aggressiveness. Displays of anger make my heart race and my insides shake, causing me to retreat into a state of protection. When threatened, I quickly shut down and I withdraw like a turtle into its shell. Feeling gagged and unable to speak because of the pain I'd seen in my parents' eyes caused by their angry exchanges. I never wanted to be the one to inflict that type of pain on anyone else, and I was afraid that because I grew up surrounded by anger, I was capable of the same kind of cruelty that I witnessed and endured. I'm not saying I haven't had my moments, but I must be pushed way beyond my limits to speak out in anger.

The word *poverty* found its place on my dominant right arm symbolizing the strength needed to cope with the embarrassment of where and how my family lived. Living in cars, motel rooms, and roach-infested trailers, wearing donated clothing, and going hungry made me uncertain whether my basic needs would be met. The inability to hide my circumstances made me a target for some of the kids I attended middle school with. I came to realize that the bullying I received for being on the Free Lunch Program at school went along with my choice to eat. As an adult, I chased moneymaking opportunities, hoping to ensure I would never be poor or hungry again.

Avoidance was one of my defense mechanisms, like an arm that could be used to push others away or to defend myself. I used it as protection against anxiety and pain by avoiding conflict, confrontations, and the unhappiness of my childhood. Sadly, the word also represents an avoidance of myself, by not acknowledging who I am out of the fear of finding out that I am insignificant, just like I felt as a child.

The legs of *molestation* and *dysfunction* created the foundation of fear and failure that followed me everywhere. Each leg represents instability on its own and together they wreak havoc on my peace of mind. The deep-seated shame I felt from being molested at ten years old supported my well-established mistrust of adults. My lower body was the central point of contact for the sexual assault I suffered at the hands of a local store owner. The programming I received as a child, such as "Respect your elders" and "Do as you are told," made me susceptible to the abuse. I told no one at the time, blamed myself for being a stupid kid that put myself in harm's way, and buried the memories of the assault.

The effect the molestation had on me as a mother was agonizing. Fear and doubt overshadowed every move I made with my firstborn son, all based on the words of a therapist who put the thought in my head that "Those who have been abused often become abusers in the same way." I was so out of touch with who I was, that I let a doctor convince me that I might be capable of harming my own child.

The dysfunction of my childhood created an inability to determine what was right and what was wrong, what was true and what was false, what was normal and what was not. I didn't know who to be or how to be. I was confused by the actions of those around me who supposedly loved each other and loved me. I learned to disassociate myself from the pain and built walls around my heart. Each new dysfunctional occurrence seemed further away from me, like a sad story I was hearing about somebody else. I buried my feelings and became numb, stuck in a mentality of unworthiness that became my comfort zone.

Once I acknowledged the pain that was stored in my body, I wanted the heaviness of the shame to be gone. The idea to "write it down" came from years of reading self-help books that encouraged me to note my issues on paper and then burn it as a sort of release. But burning the list wasn't powerful enough to purge decades of self-judgment from my nervous system. The time was long overdue for me to be honest with myself and the world around me. I was furious, and I wanted the Band-Aid of avoidance ripped off quickly.

Writing a book was a childhood dream. *How better to unearth the skeletons of my past so that I could be free of them?* I love to write. As a child, my diaries were the only safe place to express my feelings, and I continued to journal as an adult. The act of sitting in a quiet space with my journals and getting my thoughts out of my head and onto paper always made me feel better. Compiling some of my documented reflections into a book seemed like a natural way to begin to heal. By healing, I mean to move forward, not simply by reading through my past, but by feeling my way through it to get to the freedom that I knew waited for me on "the other side." Publishing the book and releasing it into the world would be my equivalent of burning the list. I've felt like a coward for most of my life. Publicly sharing my story and talking about my pain would be a chance to prove to myself that I could be courageous like the women in the Cosby trial.

The thought behind the picture on the front cover was to symbolically expose the pain points that had been hidden inside me for most of my life. I hired a local photographer and showed up with a roughly sketched drawing of the words to be placed on my body and some black crayons, the kind used at Halloween to draw clown faces or moustaches. She drew each word as instructed and took a variety of photos. Before we finished, she invited me to view the images on her computer to make sure she had captured my vision.

I finally saw her! The scared little girl who grew into a woman carrying years of emotional scars from a childhood full of chaos and instability. The photos revealed the parts of me I had determined to be unpleasant and unacceptable. Shameful weaknesses that I convinced myself would make me seem unlovable if anyone really knew. The things I didn't talk about because they make people uncomfortable. It was all there, captured forever in a photograph. Seeing the vulnerability in the image looking back at me from the screen made the pain I had denied for so long more *real*. The tears came quickly, and my heart ached with compassion.

The photographer handed me a roll of paper towels and showed me to her bathroom to wash off. Seeing that I was shaken, she gently instructed me to "take my time." I stood, in my underwear with black letters covering my pale skin, staring at what seemed to be the entirety of my life in her bathroom mirror. Tears flowing, I felt a deep sadness. A replay of how each of these pain points affected my choices in life raced through my mind. I thought about the bad decisions I'd made chasing love and acceptance. The relationships I'd chosen that were not good for my emotional well-being but felt comfortable. How fear was the driving force behind all of my actions. My sadness turned to regret and ended where the day began, in anger.

As I slowly wiped away each word with the soapy towels, it felt almost like a baptism. A cleansing of contaminated thoughts that would start me on the path of my own deconstruction.

When I received the physical pictures in the mail a few weeks later, I felt hesitant, remembering my initial reaction at the photographer's studio. I took the thin, white envelope into my home office and shut the door for privacy. In the weeks that followed the photo shoot, my emerging anger about my upbringing started to cause health issues in my gut. The inflammation of my memories manifested in a painful bout of diverticulitis, which I had never experienced before. *Was I physically and emotionally prepared to continue on this path of self-discovery?*

I held the envelope for several minutes, naively hoping the pictures would not be as emotionally provocative as they had been when I first saw them on the photographer's screen. I could feel the tension in my shoulders as I braced myself for the reveal. Finally opening the envelope, I sat in the stillness of the room and stared at her (at me). I felt each word as I read and reread them and understood the anger in her eyes. I wanted to apologize to her for being so irresponsible with her life. The longer I looked, the closer I got to accepting that she and I were one. The picture in my hand represented fifty-three years of my life. *Was the damage irreparable? Was it too late for me to take my life back?* I could see the expectation in the photo to make things right.

We all get ONE. Although the number of years we have may differ, we all get just one life. As the memories behind the pain flooded my mind, I could see how I had given pieces of my life away and how others had taken pieces of my life from me. I was afraid that becoming whole might not be possible, but if it was, I wouldn't waste any more time being less.

I wanted answers regarding some of my childhood experiences, so I decided to dig deep with close family members, asking much more personal questions than I ever had before. Nothing should be off limits to me at this point in my life. The hardest questions, though, were within me. *Who am I? What do I want? What do I do next?*

PART TWO

MEMORIES OF A CHILD IN PAIN

The mind replays what the heart can't delete.

—Unknown

3

JERSEY GIRL

My earliest memories go back to when I was around four years old. After Mom married my stepdad Lou, the four of us, Mom, Debbie, Patrick, and I, moved into his house. My new Uncle Dave stayed there with us sometimes too. It was in a small town in Camden, New Jersey, called Morgan Village. From what I remember, the house was a small cottage with a dusty, dirt-filled yard and a short picket fence that was missing some planks. Inside, the living room was sparse with red furniture, and the small eating area had a Formica-topped table with rusty metal legs and kitchen chairs with plastic seats and back cushions screwed into metal frames. There was a high chair for my little brother. At the back of the house was a tiny kitchen and bathroom. Field mice would run around inside our house, and I was afraid of them. I used to hop from the living room chair to the couch to the kitchen chair, thinking the mice couldn't get me when I was not touching the floor. My older sister and I screwed the leg off a small end table once and tried stabbing the mice with the sharp screw at the end. It didn't work; we were too slow.

Upstairs looked like an attic. The top of the stairs led straight into one big room, which was my parents' bedroom. There was a smaller room at the front of that main room where us kids slept. The two rooms were separated by a curtain in the doorway. From the top of the stairs, you could see straight through the main room, through the doorway of my room, and out the row of windows on the front of the house. As the sunlight came in through the windows, you could see the dust floating around like smoke.

Patrick's crib was in our room across from the bed that Debbie and I shared. Sometimes he was there, and sometimes he wasn't. I didn't understand it at the time, but he would be away on visits with his biological father. Debbie and I didn't visit with our biological father, and soon Patrick would not see his anymore either. I don't remember having the same curiosity as my sister Debbie had about where our biological father was. I just knew that I had a new dad.

When I was five, we moved to a small town not far from Morgan Village. The house was a twin, but much bigger than our old house. There was a porch out front that wrapped around to the front door, a fenced yard with a separate garage at the end of the driveway, and a big yard in the back. The old Victorian-style house had high ceilings and heavy wooden staircases. The living room, dining room, and kitchen all lined up in a row from front to back. Debbie and I shared a room and a bed. Patrick got his own room with a single bed and a set of bunk beds for when our cousins stayed with us. My parents' room was at the front of the house, and across from the bathroom was the staircase to the attic. I was afraid to go up there alone because the house reminded me of the haunted houses I had seen in monster movies.

Debbie and I spent our days running around the neighborhood. We'd ride our bikes down the main street to the penny candy store, be in and out of all kinds of kids' houses, steal cherries from the neighbor's tree, or play jacks on the huge set of stairs that led into the church at the end of our block. Patrick had to stay in the yard because he was so young, but occasionally he could come out with us if we were staying on our block. It's safe to say, my parents never really knew where we were, we just had to be in by dinnertime. We must have known it was dinnertime by watching when all the other kids went in.

I was a tomboy and kind of looked like Charlie Brown's friend Peppermint Patty. The kids in school would tease me about my freckles and orange hair, and because I didn't look like my brother and sister. My mother's attempts to make me look and act like a girl by insisting that I wear dresses did not stop me from crawling in the dirt underneath porches, digging for beetles and caterpillars, or wrestling around with the neighborhood boys. I'd come home covered in dirt every day.

"You're dirty and disgusting just like a little boy. When are you going to start acting like a little girl?" she'd squawk.

FEAR

Debbie, Patrick, and I started to go to a babysitter named Mrs. Joste while Mom and Dad worked. I was in kindergarten and

Debbie was in first grade. Our elementary school was around the corner from the babysitter. We walked to school each day, and Patrick was left alone with the babysitter until we got back after school.

Mrs. Joste reminded me of Humpty Dumpty with fatter legs. She was large and round and breathed heavily. Her dark brown hair was short and always wet on the back of her neck because she would sweat so much, and she was the first woman I ever saw with a moustache. She always wore a house dress with an apron and dirty flat shoes that barely held her thick feet. Her only child, Nancy, was a teenager, and her husband was a skinny old guy we didn't see much.

The house was a twin like ours, but the living and dining rooms were next to each other instead of in a row. The place was crammed with old furniture and knickknacks. You had to walk through the house single file, or you couldn't get through. It smelled old, like my grandmother's house, but with a strange odor in the dining room where all her exotic bird cages were. We were strictly instructed to stay out of the house and to keep the doors closed at all times because the change in temperature could kill the very expensive birds. When the weather kept us from going outside, we spent our time in the cold, dark basement. The room had dark brown paneling and a chocolate-colored carpet. There was a closet full of games, puzzles, and coloring books and a small table with chairs. The three of us would be down there for hours without seeing anyone else.

The Jostes had a big yard with all the fun stuff you'd find on a playground, like monkey bars, a seesaw, a swing set, and they also had a large aboveground pool. Debbie would bring her Barbies and often played alone while Patrick and I would run around jumping and swinging on everything in the yard. Patrick would pretend he was Spider-Man, and I would pretend to be Wonder Woman, and we would make up stories of people who needed to be saved by us superheroes.

Once, my brother tried to climb the monkey bars, got halfway across, and got scared.

"Just let go, I'll catch you," I begged as I stood below him with my arms open. I did not ask Debbie for help because she made it clear we were not to bother her. I was afraid to disturb Mrs. Joste as well, because she seemed angry most of the time, but he wouldn't let go and started to cry. I reluctantly ran to get the sitter's help, hoping he wouldn't slip off while I was gone. Mrs. Joste came storming outside grumbling, grabbed him by the back of his shirt, and threw him to the ground face down like a rag doll. His nose swelled up and began to bleed. She took us both inside.

"Not a word to your parents," she growled as she cleaned him up. When Mom arrived to pick us up, Patrick's nose was still swollen, and Mrs. Joste told her he had fallen. I was confused but knew I didn't want anything bad to happen to me, so I didn't say a word and neither did Patrick.

During the summer between kindergarten and first grade, Mrs. Joste adopted three siblings. Tommy and Becky, who were a little older than me, and their baby sister named Sue, who had a weird black and blue bump on her face. We were told she was sick with a hole in her heart, but she seemed like a happy baby. Her crib sat in the dining room with all those birds. I would sneak in and see baby Sue when I went into the house to use the bathroom. Sometimes, I would even ask to hold her because my mom was pregnant, and I wanted to be able to help with our new baby.

Tommy and Becky were very shy and kept to themselves. It took a little while, but they finally started to play with us, and we all became friends. They seemed like good kids, and I couldn't understand why they were getting scolded so much. While they were inside doing chores, Debbie, Patrick, and I could hear the commotion from outside. All that yelling made me feel sick and afraid, just like I felt at home sometimes.

One afternoon, Mrs. Joste shouted for Debbie and me to come into the house. We immediately ran inside, afraid we had done something wrong. The back door led straight into the kitchen, which was small and crammed with a kitchen table in the center. I often wondered how the babysitter fit in there, being as big as she was. She was ranting and raving at Tommy and Becky about something, and they looked scared.

"This is what happens when you're bad!" she shouted, pushing the table out of the way as she grabbed Tommy by the sides of his hair and started banging his head on the floor. It's hard to describe precisely what seeing such violence feels like inside a six-year-old — I was frozen with fear. "Now get outside and not a word to your parents."

We all ran for the door. Tommy came out sobbing with his nose bleeding. That would happen many times to Tommy and Becky, and each time it did, we would hear them screaming from wherever we were in the yard. I remember feeling very sad for them when they came out bleeding and crying. I was constantly worrying about doing anything wrong, trying to figure out how to be "good" so that none of that would happen to me.

Mrs. Joste would make Tommy wear his sister's dresses out in the yard after school.

"Call him Sissy, 'cause that's what he is for wetting the bed," she said, almost laughing.

Tommy was my friend and what was happening to him was horrifying, but I began to stay away from him, thinking that I'd get into trouble for not treating him the way she told us to. Ignoring Tommy made me feel even worse because he seemed so sad and scared.

We were all picked on by her teenage daughter Nancy, especially my sister Debbie. Nancy was tall, heavy, and rough-looking. She would play practical jokes on us, like giving us what looked like a drink of water that turned out to be vinegar. She would wrestle Debbie into the pool, pull her bathing suit bottoms off so she was too embarrassed to get out, and threaten to do the same to all of us. Some of us couldn't swim yet. She was a bully who pushed us around and teased us unmercifully. Going there became unbearable, yet I did not say a word to my parents about how we were treated.

Several months later, baby Sue died. At seven years old, I didn't really know what that meant and got no indication about how to feel from the stoic look on Mrs. Joste's face when she told us. She took all of us kids to the funeral home. I'm not sure if my parents ever knew that we went there; it was never mentioned. We were told to sit in chairs in the entryway as she walked into the next room. The place smelled funny, and it was very quiet. Occasionally, men dressed in suits walked through with no acknowledgement that we were there, which felt creepy. The door to the next room was propped open, and when I looked in, I saw a small white box sitting on what looked like a table.

"Come on kids, we're going in to see Susie," Mrs. Joste demanded. She looked agitated and in a hurry to do whatever she was there to do. I remember feeling a strong uncertainty. I didn't want to go in there, but I was more afraid of Mrs. Joste than what I might see in that room.

Baby Sue was lying in that tiny white box lined with silk. She was dressed in white with her arms crossed over her chest. She looked like she was sleeping, and I noticed the bump on her face was no longer black and blue.

"Say goodbye to Sue, you won't be seeing her anymore," Mrs. Joste explained without emotion. I tried not to cry but couldn't stop the tears. I had had so much fun playing with her and holding her. Now I would never see her again. Tommy and Becky stood there very still and did not cry. I was sad that they wouldn't see their little sister anymore.

I began to have nightmares. I dreamed that I was the one in the box or my pregnant mom was the one in the box and never coming back. As I lay in bed, fighting the urge to sleep, I would cross my arms over my chest just like baby Sue and imagine what it would be like to die, crying quietly so I didn't wake anyone up. I didn't know why people died, but I started to worry about everybody I loved dying and leaving me forever. The nightmares continued, and I was afraid all the time.

Mom and Dad had been trying to have a baby since they got married. It took over four years, but my younger sister Jennifer was born later that summer. I remember Dad taking us to the hospital. We weren't allowed to go in, so Mom held her up to the window of the hospital room on the third floor, and we got to see her from the sidewalk below. When Mom and Dad brought Jennifer home, it was like having a real baby doll in our house. She completed the family I grew up in. I was very happy to have a baby sister, but the nightmares about being in the box returned, and now they included Jennifer.

The weekdays were fraught with anxiousness at the babysitter's house. I never knew what to expect, and I began feeling the same way when I was home.

Mom had to have a hysterectomy not long after Jennifer was born. It was uncomfortable to be around her because she looked irritated with all of us most of the time. She was sad and angry, and her actions were unpredictable. I wasn't sure how to help, but I was worried about her.

"Just wait until your father gets home," was one of her favorite threats. If one of us was bad, we all got the belt.

"Line up," Dad would say in frustration after being trounced by my mom's bitching first thing when he walked through the door after working all day. The thought here was that we kids should police each other and keep each other in line so that none of us got in trouble. When one of us fell short, the others got disciplined as well for what Dad liked to call "GP," general principles. "This is for all the things you've done wrong that I don't know about," he'd say.

Those beatings usually happened right before we sat down to dinner. Dad would grab us by the left arm and whack us three times each, occasionally striking our hands if we involuntarily reached back to protect ourselves. That really hurt.

"Ow, ow, ow," we shrieked each time the belt hit our bottoms. I started to go first in line because Debbie would laugh in defiance sometimes when she got hit which made Dad angrier, so he hit harder. I just wanted to get it over with quickly. Then we'd all sit down to dinner on our burning bottoms and pretend like everything was fine.

"Stop crying or I'll give you something to really cry about," Dad would say if one of us happened to still be crying from getting hit. There would be silence then, except for an occasional sniffle, while I forced myself to eat.

One night, Dad came home, talked with Mom in the kitchen, then took Debbie, who was around nine years old, upstairs to our room and closed the door. There had been no warning or hint from my mom that any of us were in trouble. No "wait until your father gets home" announcement. Mom was holding my baby sister Jennifer in her arms at the bottom of the stairs looking up in silence, and I stood beside her as if we were waiting for something.

I heard Dad yelling, and then I heard the familiar "ow, ow, ow" that went along with getting the belt, but then it continued, and I heard my sister screaming for him to stop. I tried to run up the stairs to help her, but Mom grabbed my arm and held me back. I cried for my mom to help Debbie as I tried to pull away from her grip. She said nothing, and when I looked at her and pleaded with her to stop it, there was just a blank stare on her face, no emotion at all.

Debbie did not come to the dinner table, and there was nothing said about why. We sat there pretending that everything was fine as usual. Mom took dinner up and Debbie stayed in our room for the rest of the night. I was told to sleep in Patrick's room, and when I went to bed, I put my ear to the door of our bedroom but heard nothing. I couldn't understand it. None of us had ever been taken into a separate room and gotten a beating alone. *What did she do that was so bad?*

Debbie was quiet in the next few days, and we never talked about what happened. The following weekend, we were all getting ready for our monthly visit with my mom's side of the family at my grandparents' house. It was always fun seeing our aunts, uncles, and cousins, and I thought maybe that would cheer Debbie up. When I went to find her, she was in the bathtub and Mom was sitting in a chair next to it.

"Time to get out and get ready to go," Mom instructed.

Debbie was facing away from the door, and when she stood up, I saw that her entire bottom was black and blue before Mom put the towel around her. I felt a flood of emotions: sad for my sister, mad at Dad and Mom, and even more afraid for myself now that I saw the physical consequences.

When my grandmother asked my mom how Debbie had gotten the scratches on her neck, Mom said, "She fell." That seemed to be the excuse for any evidence of injury. In my fifties, I finally asked Debbie what happened. She has given me permission to tell her story.

In those days you could hear the music from the ice cream truck from a couple of blocks away. Debbie asked my mother for some money to get ice cream. Mom was napping on the couch and told her that if she found some change in the junk drawer, she could use that to get ice cream. Debbie rummaged through the junk drawer in the kitchen with no luck. She then went upstairs to my parents' room and went through their personal junk drawers, which were in the top drawers of their bureaus. She didn't find any change but found a deck of cards in a white box in my dad's drawer. She took the cards, thinking they could be stacked to make a house for her Barbies.

A few days later, Mrs. Joste's daughter Nancy had gone through Debbie's Barbie case and found the cards. She opened the box and found that the cards were white on one side but had nude pictures of women on the other side. Nancy gave them to her mother, who handed them over to my mother. I've described what happened next from my point of view.

That beating had a profound effect on me as a seven-year-old. I didn't know what Debbie had done, and that made me worry about everything I did at home from that point forward. I thought I'd better be a "good girl" because if that could happen to my sister, it could happen to me, and I couldn't count on my mom to help me.

DYSFUNCTION

When I was told that we were moving and changing babysitters, I was excited that the two and a half years of Mrs. Joste were finally coming to an end. On one of our final days there, I saw an opportunity to hurt her like she continued to hurt others. I had watched her treat her exotic birds better than she ever treated any of us kids. I snuck into the house while she was doing something outside. I left the back door open, which had a screen door, and then went and opened the front door, which sent a rush of wind through the house, blowing around the piles of feathers that were lying on the floor beneath each cage. I quickly returned outside, hoping she wouldn't catch me, feeling scared and justified.

As she approached the back door, she began to yell because it was open.

"Who left the damn kitchen door open? I've told you kids a million times not to leave any of the doors open!" She slammed the back door behind her as she entered the house, and my heart sank. Soon enough, she would see that the front door was open, too. I began to shake as I waited for her to come back outside. I made sure to stay close to the other kids, hoping they would protect me. They had seen me go inside, but I didn't tell them what I had done. Mrs. Joste never made it back outside before Mom came to get us, but I was terrified of what might happen when we got dropped off the next day.

There was no staying home if you felt sick, and I was not about to confess to any wrongdoing, so I couldn't think of any other way to get out of going to the babysitter. After my parents dropped us off, Mrs. Joste lined up my siblings and me, demanding to know who had left the doors open. She actually looked upset, and for a moment, I felt bad about what I had done. She walked over to one of the cages, uncovered it, and pulled out a dead bird.

"This is what you brats did." Her voice shook with emotion as she held the dead bird upside down by its feet. She walked into the kitchen, and we could hear her throw it in the garbage pail. The fear inside my body was intense. "Everyone outside, except for you," she growled as she pointed at me. Debbie and Patrick looked at me nervously as they headed for the back door.

"I'll give you one more chance to tell the truth."

"I didn't do it," I said, barely able to get the words out. She grabbed me by the arm and pushed me down on her recliner. Then she sat on me, and I felt like I was suffocating under her weight. The disgusting smell of her and her chair made me nauseous.

"Did you leave those doors open?" she yelled. "Tell me the truth or I won't get up."

"I'm sorry," came out as I struggled to breathe, mad at myself for breaking so easily. Mom had already ingrained in us that crying showed weakness and I felt like a coward every time I did it, but I began to cry in frustration. She got up and went on a rant about what I had done, then sent me outside. Everyone looked relieved to see me. Wiping away the tear-soaked hair that was stuck to my face, I wondered which one of them ratted me out.

We moved into an apartment for a few months, then into a townhouse in Blackwood, New Jersey. Mom started to go out, and occasionally she would take us three older kids with her and leave Dad home with Jennifer who was still a baby. My mom would take us to bars where she would meet a man and introduce him as a friend. She would put us in a booth and order each of us a Shirley Temple. Then she gave us placemats and pens that we played tic-tac-toe and connect-the-dots on while they sat at the bar. We really liked the Shirley Temples and looked forward to them on those trips.

I made sure I sat on the side of the booth where I could keep an eye on my mom. I watched her and whoever she was with intently. She was all dolled up in fancy clothes and pretty makeup, smoking a cigarette, having a drink, and smiling a lot. They would face each other on the bar stools, she would twirl her hair with her fingers, and they would laugh as they touched each other's legs. It always looked like she was having fun. When we left, she would put us in the back seat of the car and instruct us to face forward and be quiet. Then she would walk behind the car to say goodbye to her friend. We weren't supposed to look, but sometimes I did. It looked like they were kissing and hugging each other, which made me feel a pang of jealousy for my dad.

"How would you kids like a new daddy?" she asked as she turned to face us in the back seat. We just stared at her, afraid to give any reply. I did not understand. My heart sank and I felt a kind of protective panic. *Is this how you get a new dad? What's going to happen to the dad that we already have?*

ANGER

One night, Dad got so mad that Mom was out again that he put us all in the car with me in the front seat.

"Show me where she takes you," he yelled.

I was almost eight years old and had learned attention to detail. I led him to several local bars where he would run in to see if she was there while the four of us stayed in the car. It got late, and he never found her. I felt like I failed my dad.

I knew the fight was going to be a big one when Mom got home. I could see how angry Dad was. His face was red, and he sweated as he paced around. When she walked through the door all disheveled, the fighting started. Mom was a champion at fighting. She knew all the right buttons to push. Her words were her weapon of choice, and they cut like a knife. When she threatened divorce, Dad had had enough and held her up against the wall by the throat to quiet her venom. We pleaded with them to stop.

ANXIETY

I didn't know what would happen with my parents' relationship or with us. I constantly worried about one or both of them leaving, about doing the wrong thing and getting into trouble, about being the new kid as we moved around so much, and about dying because it felt like I was sick all the time. I would nervously bite my fingernails and when they got so short that they bled, I would bite my toenails.

I'm not sure why, but the six of us all moved in with my mom's parents in Cinnaminson for a while, where I went to the third school I would attend in second grade. Mom was the oldest of six kids, but the first three kids were almost adults when my grandmother had the final three kids. There were times when my grandmother and my mom were both pregnant at the same time. Another one of my mom's sisters lived right up the street and she had three sons. I liked living with my grandparents. I thought it was fun to see my aunts, uncle, and cousins every day. It made starting a new school much easier since they all went to school with us.

When I was in the middle of third grade, the six of us moved to a small town called Fairview. I remember a town square with a monument and a small park in the center that everyone called "The Square." Half the perimeter was surrounded by little stores and red brick apartment buildings. Rowhomes edged the other half. My school was on the street behind The Square and could be reached through an alleyway in the middle of the row of stores. The Lutheran Church was the first thing you saw when you crossed the little bridge into our town. Mom had taken us there for Sunday school when we first moved in. Although she did not go back, Debbie and I would dress up each Sunday morning and walk down to church on our own. It was a place where we felt safe.

TRUTH?

We used to go for Sunday drives. Our car had bench seats and no seatbelts. Mom and Dad would be in the front seat with my little sister propped on Mom's lap. She held Jennifer with one hand and a cigarette with the other. The rest of us would be in the back seat. I always had to sit between Debbie and Patrick because they didn't get along. I'd hang my arms over the front seat and listen to Mom sing along with the radio, or I'd tickle Jennifer's feet. I was amazed that Mom knew all the words to so many songs and wondered if I'd ever be able to remember songs like that.

"He's touching me," Debbie would yell in disgust.

"No, I wasn't," Patrick would rebuff.

I would be instructed to sit back so there would be no touching of anyone. On one occasion, we were driving around

Cooper River Park and Dad got so mad at the bickering that he stopped the car and let the three of us out on the side of the road. Then he drove away. We were stunned, standing there looking at each other.

"So, you think they'll come back?" I asked with my hands on my hips, as I glared at the two people guilty of getting me thrown out of the car.

We've told this story many times at family gatherings throughout the years, and my dad would assure everyone that he could see us at all times.

I wasn't a fan of the Sunday drives, but there were a couple of exceptions. In the summer, we would wear our bathing suits under our clothes, drive over, and sneak into the pool at the local Holiday Inn. Mom would pack some snacks, and we'd lounge around the pool like we were guests at the hotel. When it was time to leave, we'd just put our street clothes back on and head home, sitting on towels so we didn't get the back seat wet.

Sometimes, we would stop at model homes during our drives. There were one or two single-family show homes on the main road where a development was about to be built. The homes were empty, so they were always open for the public to go inside and look around.

"Go find your rooms," Dad would say as we entered, and we'd race each other upstairs to stake our claim on the room we wanted. The houses were much larger than anything we had ever lived in, and they were beautiful. "We're going to live in a house like this one of these days." He was a dreamer in many ways and there was a lot of stuff that was going to happen "one of these days."

On one of those Sunday drives, we stopped for breakfast. As we finished, Mom took me by the hand and told me she wanted me to meet someone. We walked over to a table where another family was having breakfast and Mom introduced me to a woman named Joan. As they stood there chatting in a whisper, I glanced around the table, noticing that a couple of the kids looked like me — redheads with freckles. We went back to our table, gathered everyone else, and left.

"Who were those people?" I asked my mother later when we were alone in my bedroom.

"That was your Aunt Joan and her family. Her brother Robert is your father." I must have looked confused because Mom continued with her story. "When I was married to Dennis, I took your sister and left him for a while because he hit me, and I wasn't putting up with that. I started dating your father and found out I was pregnant, so I went back to my marriage because it was the proper thing to do at the time. When my mother," she stumbled, "your grandmother, found out I was pregnant, she didn't think it was a good idea for me to have another child in a marriage that had troubles. She told me that there were ways to get rid of an unwanted pregnancy, like falling down the stairs or using a coat hanger, but I told her I wouldn't do that. After I had you, Dennis didn't want you girls and suggested we put you in an orphanage. There was no way I was going to let that happen, so I divorced him." Then, she quickly left the room to avoid any other questions. Mom usually did have the last word before she made her quick exits.

At eight years old, my young mind could not understand what Mom was telling me. I always thought my real dad was

Dennis Stajkowski, my older sister Debbie's biological father, the man Mom was married to when she had me, the man whose last name I had. I had never even met this guy Robert, who I was now being told was my biological father. His sister's kids, whom I saw in the restaurant, did look like me though, and I had been teased by other kids for not looking like my siblings. Although my sister and I visited with my Grandmom Stajkowski for our birthdays or holidays like Easter when she would take us out for our Easter outfits, we never visited with Dennis Stajkowski. It was all very confusing, but it sounded like nobody wanted me, and my mom saved me.

A couple of years later, Mom would explain to Debbie and me that she had made a deal with Dennis — he did not have to pay child support if he agreed never to see us and that is why there were no visits with him. I wouldn't find out until I was in my fifties that most of those stories were untrue.

ANGER

Mom started going out again and saw the same guy, Rick, for a while. He was nice when Debbie, Patrick, and I met him, but most of the time, she went out on her own. She'd come home with gifts from Rick and display them around the house. Dad was agitated on those nights home with us four kids. Thinking it would make a difference in his temper, I would help him with Jennifer since she was nearly three. They often fought when Mom came home, and the same happened when Dad came home from his nights out.

I found comfort in our pet dogs. They were mostly all German shepherd mixes, named Max, Bear, or Duke. We didn't take our pets with us when we moved. We were told they were stolen, ran away, or were going to live on a farm because we were moving. Our dogs loved me no matter what, and the love of animals was something I shared with my dad. He enjoyed walking the dogs, and I enjoyed training them. The two of us would spend time together playing fetch and goofing around with our dogs, but feeding and walking them became my responsibility as I got older.

Early one morning, Dad came charging into my room yelling and grabbed me by the hair, jolting me from sleep. I could barely comprehend what was happening as he dragged me down the steps and threw me into a pile of dog poop by the front door. He had stepped in it on his way out to work.

"Clean it up!"

I was sobbing while frantically trying to clean up the mess. I had forgotten to take Max out one last time before bed. The commotion woke the rest of the house, but no one dared come downstairs to investigate. I was hurt — not so much physically, but emotionally. I felt betrayed by my dad. His unexpected aggression toward me made me feel like I had to have my guard up around him like I had with my mother.

After cleaning up the carpet, I had to quickly clean myself before anxiously heading out to school. I smelled the dog poop on me as I sat in class and wondered if anyone else could smell it too. It reminded me all day that I had to be more careful about my chores and my dad.

I didn't sleep very well and had nights when I couldn't stop throwing up. Those were the nights that I had Mom all to myself.

She would make me hot tea and sit on the couch with my head in her lap, stroking my hair while everyone else was asleep. She would sing "You and Me Against the World," by Helen Reddy, to me. Those were some of the only nights I felt close to my mom — like she loved me. I still cry every time I hear that song.

In 1975, I was a very shy ten-year-old fifth grader. Trying to fit in more, I became a safety guard for the elementary school. My safety post was in front of the school, right at the alley that led into the town square. When school let out each day, most of the older kids would head through the alley and into The Square, and I made sure everyone crossed the street safely.

Rachel was my best friend. She was from a loud but fun Italian family. Her hair was black, and she had a big, pearly white smile. I was attracted to how lighthearted and silly she was because she helped me forget how heavy some of my days were. I'd sleep over at her house and enjoy the comforts of an attentive mother and what seemed like a normal family life. No one was allowed to sleep over at our house, or maybe I didn't ask because I didn't want my friends to feel as uncomfortable as I did at home.

Tracy was my other friend. She was much taller, with long, dirty blonde hair that was always uncombed. Their family was known throughout the neighborhood as the "poor" family. Their house was falling apart and all the kids smelled and looked unkempt. She got teased a lot in school, and I got teased for being her friend, but I felt sorry for her family. When I slept over at her house there was chaos everywhere you looked, but they all seemed oblivious to the disorder. Somehow, I felt more at home at Tracy's.

Rachel and Tracy were very different, almost opposites. I would have to spend time with one or the other. One was beautiful, and one was a tomboy like me, so the different things we did together fit each of them accordingly, meaning I had to be more of a "girl" with Rachel, and I could be more myself with Tracy.

I actually spent most of my time hanging around with my brother Patrick. We'd ride bikes, climb trees, play ball, and wander aimlessly around the neighborhood picking interesting things out of people's trash to play with. Occasionally, Debbie would grace us with her presence, but mostly she would play with her Barbies, walk her cat around the block in a wagon, or be at her friend's house. Patrick and I were too wild for her.

I had my first real crazy crush then too. His name was Daniel, and he was in the same grade. He had bright blond hair that almost looked white, thick black glasses, and a wide smile full of big white teeth. I thought he was dreamy. We'd see each other in school and meet up at the school playground on the weekends. My heart fluttered every time I saw him. We had fun running amok in the streets of our small town and hanging out in the center of The Square. Sometimes, he would buy me a slushy at the corner sandwich shop. Daniel would hold my hand, and I would blush with excitement. When he asked me if he could be my boyfriend, I almost threw up before I replied with a nervous but resounding "Yes."

The first time Daniel tried to kiss me was in the school playground. I turned like I'd seen in a movie, and his kiss landed on my cheek. We walked away giggling like we had just gotten away with something forbidden. The second time he tried to kiss me was when he was walking me home from school after my safety duties were done. We ducked into the hallway of one of the apartment buildings in The Square. I thought I was brave enough to let him kiss me on the lips, but at the last minute, I turned my head, and he got my cheek again. He was really sweet about it. He took my hand, and we giggled as he walked me home.

MOLESTATION

I would get out of my last class a little early each day to go man my safety post in front of the school. Once the flurry of kids leaving the school grounds trickled down to a few stragglers, the head safety would yell, "Off!" and we were excused to head home ourselves. By the time I arrived at The Square, most of the other kids had made their way through and it was quiet.

There was a five-and-dime store next to the sandwich shop. It was a store full of odds and ends, like today's dollar stores, except much smaller. They had a big candy rack right inside the front door, and that was the stop for most of the kids filtering through The Square each day. I was no exception, but all I did was go in and look at the candy. I'd stand there and pick out, in my mind, what I would get if I had any money. The $100,000 Bars, Charleston Chews, and Chuckles were my favorites, but most of the time I'd leave empty-handed unless I had gotten some quarters taped in a card from my Great Grandmom Schard or my Grandmom Stajkowski.

We lived in Fairview for about two and a half years, which was longer than in other places. Most people were friendly; you got to know them, and they got to know you. The five-and-dime store was owned by two brothers who looked as old as my granddad. I knew they were brothers because I had been in the store a few times with Mom when we first moved there, and I overheard her talking with them.

Back in those days, your parents would send you to the store with some money and a note listing what they wanted, and the store owners would help you gather the items. As I got a little older, I got used to going into stores alone.

On one of my usual stops after school, one of the owners asked, "Why do you come in here every day to look at the candy but never buy any?"

"I don't have any money."

"Why don't you ask your parents? They've sent you in here before."

"They don't have any money for candy," I explained.

My parents fought constantly about money, and I often heard reminders like "We can't afford that" or "We don't have the money for that." So, I knew not to ask them for money to buy anything.

"Do you want a job? You could make some money and have all the candy you want."

I knew that other kids mowed lawns and babysat, so it seemed okay that I could have a job. I felt like I knew both the owners because I had shopped there on occasion with a list from my parents. When he told me I could make money and that I could have all the candy I wanted, it seemed like a dream come true.

"Yes, I think that would be okay."

"My name is Mr. Harper. You come see me after school tomorrow, then."

I headed home, skipping and doing cartwheels, feeling like a big girl. I would do anything to help my family and to get all the free candy I wanted, or probably the other way around, given the priorities of a ten-year-old. Mom was still working in an office, and Dad was still working in a warehouse, so they wouldn't know what I did after school. Jennifer was the only one still going to a babysitter. Debbie, Patrick, and I did our own things after school, like riding bikes or visiting friends. I couldn't wait to surprise my parents with all the money I was going to make. I desperately wanted their attention and approval. *Maybe this would be something they could be proud of me for, and they'd stop fighting about money.*

I went to the store the next day after my duties as school safety were over. There was nobody in the store except Mr. Harper and me, but that didn't seem odd; there usually wasn't anyone in there when I stopped to look at the candy.

"Let's talk about what you know how to do, and I'll find a job for you," he said as he led me to the back of the store.

We headed toward a heavy wooden chair tucked back by the racks of greeting cards. It was out of sight of the front door. He sat down with his legs open and pulled me in as if he wanted me to sit on his knee, but he left me standing. He had one arm around my waist, which made me nervous, but I was taught to respect my elders and do as I was told. He asked me about the chores I did at home — if I swept floors or dusted shelves. I began to calm down a little, and it started to feel like I was talking to my granddad.

"Do you have a boyfriend?" he asked. That made me giggle a little and blush, which gave away my secret crush. "Has your boyfriend kissed you?"

I quickly said, "No." I was beginning to feel nervous again, with a warmth in my face that felt like embarrassment. He was sweating and breathing heavily.

"If you really like this boy, there are some things you could do to make him happy so that he will keep being your boyfriend. I can show you what boys want from girls." His grasp on me tightened. I wanted to leave. I was afraid and tried to turn toward the door, frantically realizing that I could not see the door but hoping someone would come into the store. *Please someone come in the door!*

He moved his other hand under my shirt and up toward my chest. My body shook uncontrollably, and tears filled my eyes. His breath smelled like smoke, and he was talking in a perverted whisper about what boys liked to do to girls as he pinched at the tiny bumps that were my breasts — my body stiffened in disbelief.

"Girls need to let boys do what they want," he groaned as he slowly removed his hand from my shirt and unbuttoned and unzipped my pants. He spread my legs with his foot and put his hand in my underpants. He started rubbing my vagina and then shoved his finger inside me. "Does that feel good?" he asked in an evil whisper. I tried to close my legs and wiggle my way out of his grasp. He struggled to keep me still while telling me over and over that this is what you have to let boys do, this is what they want. His hand started moving back and forth faster. He breathed harder and got rougher as he stuck two fingers inside me. It hurt, just like the time I was climbing the kitchen cabinets to get something from up top and fell onto the open door of the lower cabinet and had to go to the hospital.

All my senses were alert. My head listened to what he was saying, my body shook in fear as he held me tighter, and my vagina felt pain. Tears ran down my face. I wanted to scream, but I couldn't make a sound.

I'm not sure how long the first sexual abuse lasted, but he suddenly took his hand out of my pants, stood up, and started walking to the front of the store. I zipped up my pants and followed.

"Take whatever you want," he said as he stopped in front of the rack of candy, blocking the front door. "Come back tomorrow so you can start your job."

I grabbed a $100,000 Bar and ran straight home, relieved to see that my siblings were not there. I put it on the table for my sister or brother to eat and went to my room. I was shaking and crying but didn't want anyone else to see me when they came home. I felt like I had done something bad. I had never been touched like that before, but by now, I thought that adults were allowed to do anything they wanted to do to kids.

It was hard for me to sleep. I thought about what had happened. I wondered if I would get in trouble for not going back to do the job I agreed to take. Mom and Dad often talked about how important it was not to miss work. I thought about the money I could make to help my parents.

The next day, I did the unthinkable. Although I was scared, I went back. I thought I had to since Mr. Harper said he had a job for me, and he told me to come back. I wanted to make money so my parents wouldn't fight about it so much; maybe they would even stop talking about getting divorced. I wanted to help my family stay together. I wanted to do something Mom would be proud of.

He greeted me like a friend at the front of the store — as if nothing had happened. I looked around, hoping other people were in the store, but I saw no one.

"I'm going to have you sweep up the stock room," he said as he motioned toward the back of the store. "The dustpan and broom are back here."

For a moment, I felt okay as we walked toward the back of the store. I was ready to work. When we got closer to the chair near the card racks, he grabbed my arm and pulled me into the same position as the day before.

"Let's talk a little more before you get started," he said. I stiffened up and began to shake, bracing myself for whatever was going to happen. He held me there exactly like the day before, again helping himself to my innocence.

I desperately hoped someone would come in the front door and stop what he was doing to me. I tried fighting my way out of his grasp, crying again, and this time the words came freely, "I want to leave!"

He held tighter, the struggle making him more excited, "You must like what I am doing, you came back."

"No! I want to leave!" I pleaded.

"If you tell anyone, no one will believe you. They will think you're a lying little brat, and you will get into trouble." Hearing that, I gave up. *It's all my fault. I shouldn't have come back.* When he was done, he pushed me aside and walked to the front door, again offering me anything I wanted on the candy rack. I ran past him and all the way home, hoping no one would see me. I hid in a corner of our dark basement to cry so that my sister and brother would not hear me. I was mad at myself for going back there and physically hurt by his manhandling.

I never went back to that store again. I wouldn't even walk by it for fear that Mr. Harper would come out and grab me. I began to shake if I even got within sight of it. I never told anyone what happened. I was afraid of getting into trouble at home, like he said, considering what happened just a few weeks prior.

My dog Max had followed me to school one day. A teacher told me to take him home and come back to school. I called Mom at work when I got home to tell her what happened, and she told me just to stay home. The vice-principal, Mrs. Watkins, came to my house, picked me up, and took me back to school. As I entered the school, the principal, Mrs. Brennan, was at the other end of the hallway screaming at me for not coming back to school on my own. She grabbed me by the arm, dragged me to my gym class, and made a huge scene in front of the entire class. I couldn't help crying. She told me to stop being a baby, and she hoped I had learned a lesson. The heat in my face gave away my embarrassment.

Later that night, my parents took Mrs. Brennan's side. I got yelled at and grounded, even though Mom had told me to stay home. So, I thought if I told them what happened at the five-and-dime store, they would take his side, and the punishment might be worse. Although I craved their consolation, I did not say a word about what happened.

A week or so after the abuse in the store, Daniel met me at the school playground like we had been doing since our little crush began. We were goofing around, and he got me on the ground. It was normal for us to wrestle. He straddled my belly and held my wrists down. He was laughing and trying to kiss me on the lips.

"Get off me," I yelled in a panic as I shook my head back and forth so he would get my cheek like the other two times he had tried to kiss me, but he finally caught me on the lips. He jumped up, laughing with his arms raised in victory. I got up and ran home. I didn't like him anymore after that.

Nightmares that the store owner was coming to get me kept me up. The things he said to me repeated over and over in my head. I would wrap myself up in blankets, always making sure my private parts were covered tightly while I slept. My mother wouldn't even talk to my sister Debbie and me about our periods or what was happening with our bodies as we grew. My sister and I would talk about that stuff in our closet, thinking it was dirty or forbidden. So, I couldn't talk to Mom about the aroused feelings that were awakened in my body way too early by the abuse. I kept it all to myself, feeling confused and ashamed.

I wouldn't understand the power of shame until more than forty years later while watching the Bill Cosby trial. How it's designed to keep victims quiet and to protect abusers. Planting the seed of wrongdoing in the soul of the abused, convincing us that the pain we've buried was self-inflicted by our own choices.

Two older ladies in our town created a girls' clubhouse on the second floor of one of the shops in The Square. Mrs. Kraus was short and round, with her salt and pepper hair always bobby pinned in curls on the back of her head. She was more outspoken than Mrs. Duncan, who was a little taller with a full head of gray hair teased out in a short hairdo like my Great Grandmom Schard's. If you were a girl, you could hang out there on Friday nights. There were board games, a ping-pong table, a jukebox, and a few couches to lounge on. They taught us how to line dance and gave us advice on how to be nice young ladies. It was like having two extra grandmas, and I loved going there. I felt safe there and wanted to tell them what happened to me in the store, hoping they could explain the things that were done, what I heard, and what I was feeling, but ultimately, I was too afraid to say anything.

The ladies planned a dance to celebrate the end of the school year, and we were allowed to ask a boy to go with us if we wanted to. My best friend Rachel was taking someone, and she expected me to do the same. I was sad that I would not be going with Daniel but decided to ask another kid, nicknamed Franken-stein. We called him that because his name was Frank and he had a very big forehead that protruded out over his eyes, and dark circles under his eyes. Frank was cute in his own way. I passed him a note in class, hoping to avoid the face-to-face rejection I anticipated — after all, I now had a dirty secret and thought no one would like me if they found out.

"Yes," Frank said as he approached me at my safety post. I felt my face heat up and butterflies in my stomach. He had a sweet smile on his face that would make any girl melt with adoration.

We got dressed for the dance at Rachel's house. I didn't have any fancy dresses, so I borrowed one from her. It was a very short, sleeveless white dress with a wavy bottom and a thick red line along the hem. The polyester felt itchy on my skin. I also had to borrow her white shoes, which were too big, so I stuffed napkins in the toes. I felt half naked in that dress and very uncomfortable, wishing I could just go in jeans, a T-shirt, and some sneakers.

Rachel and I walked to The Square, and the boys were waiting for us at the clubhouse. My feet hurt and I pulled down at the bottom of the dress, worried that my underpants could be seen if the wind blew hard enough. As soon as Frank saw me, he told me I looked pretty and that made all the dressing up worth it.

Mrs. Kraus and Mrs. Duncan were also in fancy dresses and had decorated the clubhouse with balloons and streamers in our school colors. They made a bunch of cookies and brownies to go along with the chips and pretzels. We played games, listened to music, and talked about what we would be doing over the summer. The ping-pong table was pushed aside to make a dance floor, where they tried to teach us how to slow dance with the boys. I'm not sure who laughed more, us girls, the boys, or the two of them, but what fun we all had.

After the dance, Rachel and I, along with our dates, headed down to the sandwich shop on the corner. I was relieved to see the five-and-dime store was closed as we passed by. We sat in a booth, drinking slushies, laughing, and teasing each other about the slow-dancing lessons. At the end of the night, we all said goodbye, and I walked home with my older sister Debbie, who had been at the dance too. I had only just turned eleven, and this was my first official date. Frank showed me he was a nice boy. He didn't try to kiss me or do anything to me that would hurt me. I was surprised that I liked him. We had a lot of fun, and it makes me smile whenever I think about him and that night.

NOT GOOD ENOUGH

A few days later, I graduated from elementary school, number two in my class. I had worked hard to get good grades, hoping my parents would be proud of me. I was barely beaten out by my nemesis, Darlene. We were neck and neck all year. The top five students had to read parts of a speech up on stage at graduation, so I made sure I dressed in my nicest casual clothes. The principal lined us up on stage in order of our rank, revealing to everyone that I was number two. As I stood on stage in front of an auditorium full of people, I nervously looked out into the crowd for my parents, but my eyes couldn't spot them. Right before it was my turn to speak, I realized I was still chewing gum and imagined it flying out of my mouth when I spoke. My voice cracked, and I hardly got the words out while trying to hold the gum in. I felt as if everyone was judging my rank, the way I looked, and the way I sounded, which made me flush with embarrassment.

On the way home, Mom let me know how disappointed she was that I had come in second by talking about how proud Darlene's parents must be of her and how she must have worked harder than me. I felt defeated, but I was determined not to let her see that. Dad was always good for a "Way to go, kid."

DYSFUNCTION

Not long after that, we had a yard sale, packed up the car with whatever could fit beside the six of us, and moved to Florida. We each got to pick one important thing to take, and since our dog Max had mysteriously run away from home, I took my diaries. The car was packed so tightly that we had to stop at a dumpster somewhere between New Jersey and Florida to toss more of the things weighing our Chevy down. I don't know exactly what was thrown out, but I made sure to hang on to my diaries.

We had driven to Florida before on vacation with my mom's parents and her younger siblings. My parents sold this move to us as an adventure, and they seemed optimistic about starting over once again. We played car games on the ride, like the first one seeing a palm tree or the giant statue at the South of the Border shops would win a quarter. I remember stopping a lot for Jennifer to use the bathroom since she was three and newly potty-trained. As usual, I was sitting between Debbie and Patrick in the back seat, but this time we were crammed back there with bags of clothing. Everyone was touching everyone, and there was little room to maneuver when I got elbowed and ordered to "move over."

Surprise relocations and leaving our friends and belongings behind were becoming commonplace and would continue to be the norm. Moving was always sad. I couldn't help thinking about Rachel, Tracy, and my new crush on Frank though. We had only seen each other in school after the dance, but I knew that if I had stayed, I would have wanted to see him more. I wanted to write about how I was feeling in my diary, but there was no way I was pulling it out while I was crushed between Debbie and Patrick. I closed my eyes and enjoyed getting lost in a daydream about seeing Frank again one day if we ever moved back.

HEADED SOUTH

I overheard Mom and Dad talking about the economy being bad and unemployment being on the rise. During the drive down, they had been promised jobs in Tampa by a man they met when we were there on vacation and were expecting those jobs and a place to stay when we arrived. I learned to listen or eavesdrop on their conversations in an attempt to gauge their moods and to find out what was happening next so that I wouldn't be surprised by either. It sounded like they were still optimistic, which eased my worry.

When we arrived in Tampa, we stopped at someone's house to pick up the keys to our new home. Mom and Dad stood outside the car, talking with the guy for a bit before he handed over the keys. On our way over to the house, Dad drove us by the animal safari section of Busch Gardens, which was only a few blocks away from where we would live. I saw a giraffe and thought it was cool that I'd be living near a bunch of wild animals.

We pulled up to a house that looked as big as some of the model homes we used to run through on our Sunday drives, and I got excited. *We finally get to live in a big house*! Dad opened the door, and we all rushed in to claim our bedrooms. There was a master bedroom on one side of the house; the kitchen, living room, and bathroom were in the center of the house; and there were two other bedrooms on the other side. The master bedroom had a bed, the kitchen had a table, and the living room had a couch. That was the only furniture in the whole place. I was confused because the house looked big on the outside, but small on the inside. Mom opened windows as we all reconvened in the living room for further instructions from my dad, beads of sweat running down all our faces.

I noticed my parents glancing at each other, looking more concerned than they had on the ride down.

"This house is split into a few apartments, and a woman is living in one of them with her son," Dad explained. Although the words were not said, his message that we were to behave and respect the others living on the property was understood. "Let's get everything out of the car, and then we'll take a look around."

It didn't take long for us to unload the large, black trash bags full of stuff. We piled them all in the living room before rummaging around for our things. Jennifer was small at three, but wanted to help, so I dug shoes out of a bag for her to carry to the master bedroom. The two other bedrooms looked exactly the same, small and empty. Debbie and I threw our stuff in one, and Patrick got the other.

I was curious to see the rest of the property. When we finished dividing up the bags, I reminded Dad to show us around. We walked around to the back of the house, where a small yard led into the woods. Dad unlocked the door to what he called "the basement apartment." The space was one big room with a small kitchenette at one end. There was a small, round table by the kitchen and a large waterbed in the center of the room as you walked in the door. It was colder down there, which felt nice. Then we walked around to the other side of the house and saw the door leading to the occupied apartment.

POVERTY

The jobs that had been promised to my parents did not pan out and they had a hard time finding work. Debbie, Patrick, and I would explore the wide-open spaces that surrounded the house during the day, while my parents took turns looking for jobs and watching Jennifer. At night, Mom, Dad, and Jennifer slept in the master, and the rest of us slept on the floors in our rooms. Although I was glad that we had moved far away from the five-and-dime store, the distance did not help me forget, and the nightmares continued.

One night Mom and Dad let us three older kids sleep on the waterbed down in the basement apartment. Dad locked us in the apartment for the night, and we put Patrick in the middle since he was the youngest. The waterbed was much more comfortable than sleeping on the floor.

I woke up the next morning to my sister Debbie screaming.

"You are disgusting! I hate you!" she shouted at Patrick as she stood by the bed covered in vomit. Who knew that Patrick's motion sickness would affect him on a waterbed? I thought that was hilarious but felt bad for Patrick as he crumbled under the weight of my sister's meltdown. I think that was the only time we got to sleep down there.

The roaches were everywhere and got into everything. I vividly remember climbing up on a chair to get a box of cereal out of the cabinet above the refrigerator one day, pouring myself a bowl, adding milk, and eating the cereal. When Mom walked into the kitchen, I asked what the little oblong things were that were left floating in the milk. She gasped, "Those are roach eggs!"

I immediately felt sick to my stomach. "Can you die from eating roach eggs?"

She grabbed the cereal box, looked inside, and then casually tossed it in the trash. "You'll be fine."

I went in the bathroom to stick my finger down my throat, but I hated throwing up, so I just sat there on the bathroom floor until the queasiness went away. There wasn't much food around, but I thoroughly examined everything I ate from that point forward.

Mom finally took a job as an assistant manager at a Waffle House, but Dad continued to struggle to find a job. They started arguing more, and I felt the continuous tension between them. Back in New Jersey, we had been a middle-class family that struggled to make ends meet but had all our basic "material" needs met. The next few years would be different.

My time in Florida would include sixth and seventh grades in four different schools and six different places to live, not counting the several days we lived in our car. There were a couple of rental houses and several trailers. Each was sparsely furnished, and roach infested.

The continuous moving made me feel like I didn't belong anywhere. For someone as shy as I was, starting new schools and being the center of attention was excruciating. All I wanted to do was hide.

My Grandmom Stajkowski had moved to Florida a few years prior. Debbie and I would spend weekends with her a couple of times a month. There, we got to sleep in a nice bed and eat as much as we wanted. She had air conditioning and there was a pool in her community that made me forget about the Florida heat. Debbie and Grandmom would sit together chatting while I chased little lizards and splashed around in the pool. We enjoyed the time we spent with her; it was a nice break from being at home.

One of the tiny rental houses in Tampa was a two-bedroom house made of cinder blocks painted bright, tropical, beach-town green. Inside was a couch, a chair, and a TV in the living room, a single bed in one bedroom, and nothing in the other. There was one bathroom and a small kitchen.

To our surprise, we found a stray dog in the garage who growled and snapped at us. Mom said I could keep him, so I named him Sammy and got to work on making him a friend. Sammy was a smaller white dog with brown and black spots, and he looked scared. I would enter the garage slowly with some small pieces of bologna in hand and sit on the step just inside the garage door. Sammy was usually curled up in one of the far corners of the garage, shaking. I would hold out my hand with a piece of bologna and quietly call him over. If anyone else in my family tried to go in the garage, he'd growl and snap like he did when we first moved in. It took a week or two of spending time with him in the garage before I could trust him in the house with everyone else, or more likely, before he would trust them. I was only bitten hard enough to bleed once while training him, but we all knew that unless you were bleeding heavily or a limb was hanging off, there was no crying and no sympathy.

Dad had taken a job as a security guard and was gone most of the day. Mom's shift at the Waffle House started later in the afternoon, leaving the four of us kids home alone for an hour or so before Dad's workday ended. We all rotated between sleeping in the single bed, on the couch, and on the chair. My parents got the first choice of where they were sleeping, and the rest of us filled in the spots that were left. I preferred the chair or the floor in the empty second bedroom because I was restless and often woke up at night.

The TV was damaged; everything we watched was green. Mom came up with the idea of building a makeshift kitchen table out of the cinder blocks and paneling she found in the garage. Debbie, Patrick, and I helped her lug the pieces into the kitchen, and we stacked them together. Mom used the table for preparation because there were no chairs and counter space was limited. My parents always encouraged us to "make do with what you have," and there were plenty of opportunities to come up with creative ideas for solving problems.

My family lived on fried bologna, Spam, and grits cooked on a hotplate — we didn't have the money to turn on the gas for the stove. Our clothes came from Goodwill, and some things had to be worn twice a week. We washed them in the bathtub with dish soap and hung them on a clothesline in the yard to dry. The trees that held the clothesline were great for climbing, and sometimes I got distracted from that chore, finding solitude and peace amongst the branches. If I was missing too long, Patrick knew where to find me.

That first winter in Florida, it snowed for the first time in years, and they closed the schools. The news covered all kinds of accidents caused by the weather. We thought it was funny coming from living in New Jersey, where it snowed for real.

A day off from school meant we didn't eat very much, and that was no laughing matter. My siblings and I got teased in school for being on the Free Lunch Program, for our clothes, and for how we looked and smelled. My family started to remind me of my friend Tracy's family back in Fairview. I wondered if people judged us to be the "poor" family now.

I got in my first fistfight at the bus stop in sixth grade. Each day, the same boy would pick on Patrick and me. After school one day, he took my school bag and threw my books and homework all over the ground. My schoolwork and grades were extremely important to me, and now my hard work was flying around everywhere. I'd had enough and tackled the kid to the ground, pummeling him until he broke free and ran away, releasing the pent-up embarrassment and frustration I felt about my circumstances. Patrick and I gathered all my schoolwork that hadn't blown away and walked home. The things that happened to us kids were never discussed with our parents or even between ourselves most of the time. My parents were always so distracted by their own issues. That boy never bothered us again, though.

The lack of money continued to put a strain on my parents. Dad worked part-time at several odd jobs when he could, which left them strapped. When Dad wasn't working, he would pick us up from school and take us for walks in the thick, prickly brush along the busy main streets. Using garbage bags, we would collect bottles that had been thrown out of car windows into the brush. The bottles could be returned to the store for a refund of five or ten cents each.

On Thanksgiving, we were getting ready to have the usual, fried bologna and grits. In the past, we shared holidays with our relatives and there was always more than enough food, but since we moved so far away, this year would not be the same. There was a knock at the door, and when I opened it, several people were standing there.

"Are your parents home, honey?"

I called my dad to the door.

"Hello, Mr. McConnell, my name is Pastor Scott. We are from Trinity Lutheran, right up the street. A couple of us were in the Waffle House your wife works at about a week ago and overheard a conversation about the hardships your family is currently experiencing. I hope you don't mind, but we asked one of the waitresses for your address so that we could help you with the holidays. We brought your family a Thanksgiving dinner with all the side dishes and dessert. Would you like us to bring it in?"

Mom had approached the door halfway through the conversation and politely responded to the Pastor's question with a "Yes, thank you," looking deserving of God's graces. Dad's face was red, and he looked uncomfortable, even somewhat embarrassed. My siblings and I were huddled together, wide-eyed, as we watched the parade of food they brought in. It looked and smelled heavenly!

"We also took up a small collection," the Pastor stopped and added as the group was leaving. He gave the money to my dad and shook his hand.

Dad swallowed hard, and his voice cracked, "Thank you and Happy Thanksgiving."

"Happy Thanksgiving," Mom yelled from the kitchen, already unpacking the food we received.

"God bless you and your family, sir. Happy Thanksgiving." The pastor left, joining the rest of the group already outside. That was the first time I ever saw my dad cry.

We feasted, sitting on the floor around the plywood table, and gave thanks to God for looking out for us. Mom was brought up a believer and would thank God often. Even though my parents did not attend church, they encouraged us to help others whenever we could, just like the church group had helped us. I would catch Mom putting change in the donation can at the cash register in a store, even though we didn't have much. Debbie and I continued to find a way to make it to Sunday school wherever we were living. Going to church gave us hope that things would get better, and we got snacks. If our parents couldn't take care of us, we believed that God would.

Christmas came quickly, and we were told there would be no presents. The Waffle House employees were throwing a Christmas party, and we all got to go. The employees' kids stayed in somebody's house with a babysitter while the adults attended the party in the community clubhouse nearby. The house was decorated with Christmas lights, a manger, and a big tree with a pile of presents under it. Santa, Mrs. Claus, and Rudolph figures graced the front lawn.

We used to have Christmases like that in New Jersey, but back at our house, sitting on top of the TV, stood a one-foot-high plastic tree with eight tiny Christmas balls that Mom got at the dollar store.

After we ate as much food as we could, Debbie, Patrick, and I took Jennifer over to see the beautiful Christmas tree. We couldn't help but look at the packages underneath and thought it was odd that our names were on the presents. Nervously, we asked around to see if any of the other kids had the same names, and they did not. We talked amongst ourselves about the possibility that the presents might be for us, feeling cautiously excited. *Were my parents kidding about there being no presents this year?*

When it was time to go home, the owners of the house told my parents that the gifts were for us. Employees at four different Waffle House locations had each taken one of our names and bought us Christmas presents. My parents started to load the colorfully wrapped boxes into our car. From the back seat we could see Dad shaking hands with Mom's coworkers as Mom smiled and expressed her gratitude. We were obnoxiously giddy.

Although most of the presents were practical, like clothing, shoes, and school supplies, it was nice to have new things, not used or handed down. I got a shirt that had bright, different-colored horizontal stripes that I just loved. That shirt would be the reason I got into my second fistfight. At the trailer park we moved to next, I lent it to a friend, and she refused to give it back. I lost a toenail in that fight that started inside the trailer and ended in the middle of our gravel road. That shirt was important to me

— a heartfelt gift from strangers who wanted me to have a Merry Christmas. I made sure I got it back.

Between that trailer and the next, we lived out of our car for a few days. Mom and Dad registered us in a new school so that we could eat and basically be babysat while they looked for our next home. It was the middle of seventh grade for me, and I was the new kid again. In art class, we learned how to make a home-made camera on my first day there. We went outside and took pictures of the trees and the playground. The next day, we learned how to develop the pictures we had taken. I enjoyed that class. After two days, we moved on.

The last place we lived in Florida was a trailer inside a big fenced-in yard. The owners lived in another trailer on the property. They had ten chihuahuas that ran around barking all day long, a bunch of chicken coops behind the trailer we lived in, and a cow behind their trailer. The smell of that many animals in the Florida heat was disgusting. The cockroaches were everywhere, and at night, I would wrap myself up from head to toe while I slept with only a slit open to breathe. I kept my hand over my mouth to feel if any roaches got close because they would crawl all over us. Palmetto bugs, which are much larger flying roach-type bugs, would also come out at night. I could hear them hitting the walls and windows as I lay in bed. If I had to get up, I always made sure I put shoes on so I wouldn't step on the bugs, checking that there were none inside my shoes first.

It would be nothing to take a glass out of the cabinet and have a roach egg laying in the bottom or to open the silverware drawer and see the roaches scatter. I picked up a habit of rinsing everything off in the kitchen sink before I used it. I catch myself doing that to this day, even in my own house, where there are no bugs.

That property had a huge tree right in the middle that was great for climbing and sitting in to get away from all those yappy dogs. It became a nice place for me to escape the chaos in our house and hide from everyone. My boyfriend David's house was right across the road, and I could see it from the tree. Sometimes, he joined me up there. I also had some friends from school who lived close enough to come play baseball in the open field next door. I'd spend as much time as I could outside or at friends' houses to avoid our living conditions.

My family lived in that trailer for several months, and when school let out for summer vacation, Mom gave us a week's notice that we were moving to Louisiana. She explained that there were better job opportunities there and that we would be better off moving than staying in Florida where the job market was so bad. At least I had enough time to say goodbye to a few friends and my boyfriend, David.

A week later, we drove to Louisiana. Again, we were each allowed to take one item and some clothes. I always chose my diaries; they were my best friends, where I shared my feelings and fears, and where my life — and what I thought — mattered.

BETTER DAYS AHEAD

We moved to Louisiana with a coworker of Mom's named Sharon and her two kids, Becky and Joe, who were eight and eleven. Mom and Sharon arranged to work at a Waffle House together in Baton Rouge, and Dad quickly got a warehouse job. The nine of us lived in a motel room for our first six months there. Two beds and a kitchenette for three adults and six kids aged six to fifteen. Sharon and her kids would sleep in one bed, Mom, Dad, and Jennifer would sleep in the other bed, and Debbie, Patrick, and I would sleep on the floor. We older kids would spend most of our time outside, running around the motel and playing in the drained pool, while Jennifer and Becky stayed with Mom or Sharon. Every day was chaos, especially when we went back to school. My parents grew very impatient and frustrated with our situation.

After the motel, our family moved into a furnished three bedroom, one-bath rental house. The house was a rancher with all the bedrooms on one side of the house, the kitchen and living room in the middle, and a garage that was converted into a family room on the other side. Surprisingly, a stray dog was left in that house too. She was a sweet little dog with brindle coloring. Mom said I could keep her. I named her Runt because she was so small.

The neighborhood was more like New Jersey than Florida in that the houses were much closer together and the area was more populated. The school bus stops were crowded and closer together, and the bus ride was shorter. All that made it easier to make new friends. Of course, the thick Southern accents everyone had were nothing like what I heard in New Jersey or Florida.

Living in Louisiana was very different from living up north. Kids under eighteen were getting married and having babies. Segregation was evident. I was permitted to start working at thirteen and driving at fourteen. People rode horses wherever they wanted.

We even experienced our first tornado as it whizzed down our street; we taped the windows with a big X and sheltered in closets, like we'd seen people do in the movies. Whenever stronger hurricanes were predicted to hit, families from the Gulf Coast would travel inland to seek shelter. A couple of times, random families knocked at our door and asked to ride out the storm with us. Our door was always open, and it wasn't a surprise to find strangers in our house when we woke up some mornings. My parents were always willing to help others in need.

The couple of years we lived in Louisiana were fun because I had more opportunities to get out of the house. Mom was a manager at the Waffle House, and Debbie and I went to work for her. Dad would drive the three of us to work at 5:00 a.m. on the weekends. He would sit and have breakfast with us before heading back home to be with Patrick and Jennifer, who were still in bed. I worked as a dishwasher before quickly moving up to waitressing. I didn't mind handing over my earnings to help with the bills at home if they let me keep enough to go to the skating rink every Friday night and out with my friends.

My parents were still barely getting by even though Dad had a steady warehouse job and Mom, Debbie, and I worked at the Waffle House. They still fought about money often, but life wasn't as destitute as it had been in Florida. I couldn't understand why my mom was taking more medications and having panic attacks, but I began to worry about her more.

Since Mom was the manager, if someone called in sick or went home early on the weekends, my sister Debbie and I filled in, even pulling some doubles or all-nighters if needed. Those overnight shifts were wild and crazy. Rowdy customers would come in drunk from the bars and have races with the high chairs or moon us from the parking lot and leave their butt cheek marks on the fogged windows. Occasionally, there would be a full-out brawl that would start inside the diner then quickly become a mob scene outside in the parking lot. That was especially worrisome because some customers carried weapons.

My parents became friendly with one of the customers named Derrick. He reminded me of Sam Elliott, except with dirty blond hair. Derrick was a cowboy, and when he stayed with us, he parked his horse in our backyard. He was an American Quarter Horse, and he was beautiful. Derrick let us ride him, and that's when I fell in love with horses.

The neighbor didn't like that we had a horse in the backyard. Their little yappy dog would bark excessively at the horse who would then put his head over our fence to check out what was making all the noise, nudging the dog with his nose. The police came to the door one afternoon when my parents were working because of a complaint from that neighbor. While my sister was talking with them at the front door, I tried to get the horse in the house through the back door to hide it. Leading a horse through a kitchen door isn't as easy as it sounds. Needless to say, the horse did not cooperate. The police left us with a warning and went on their way.

I have no idea why, but we moved into an apartment complex after that house. Fortunately, I got to stay in the same middle school for two years straight. I had a group of good friends, worked on the school newspaper, had fun at work, and had new and different experiences. I went to rodeos, rode on ATVs and motorcycles, raced around a lake on a speedboat, was taught to drive a stick shift in what looked to me like a monster truck by a friend of my parents, raced with my friends on horseback, and went to an actual disco like the one in Saturday Night Fever. At fifteen years old, I began to enjoy my social life as an escape from whatever drama was happening at home.

I met a lot of people working at the Waffle House, both customers and coworkers. One of the hot skate guards from the roller-skating rink came in for breakfast every Saturday with his dad, and I would get absolutely dizzy with excitement. When they sat in my section, I could barely take their order without feeling like I would faint. Chuck was tall, dark, and incredibly handsome. He had a very charming nature and spoke smoothly, like butter.

Chuck asked me out once and came over to my house after school to pick me up. I could hardly believe he was in my house, let alone taking me on a date. We sat on the couch together, waiting for my parents to get home because I was babysitting Patrick and Jennifer. When Dad came through the door and saw us, he took his big wad of keys and threw them at me, hitting me in the back. Then he threw Chuck out. I was mortified and avoided going to the skating rink that Friday night because I couldn't face him. When he came into the Waffle House for breakfast with his dad that Saturday morning, I let someone else wait on them. I mustered enough courage to tell him I was sorry about what happened though.

Chuck was eighteen, with a full mustache, and dark hair, eyes, and complexion. My dad did not approve of some of the boys I liked. They were usually older, with a brooding temperament, and an air of cockiness. Since I learned how to be such a good girl, my eye was always on the "bad boy" types.

6

RETURN TO FAMILY

The summer before I was set to move up to the high school for tenth grade, we traveled back to New Jersey for a two-week vacation to see my grandparents. We stayed with my great-grandmother in Philadelphia. She was my mom's grandmother on her mother's side, and we called her Gram. Mom had a much better relationship with her than her own mother, and so did we. She was a short, staunch German lady in a house dress and apron with teased-out granny hair that looked like a helmet. Although Gram looked intimidating and mean, she had a soft side. When she smiled, which wasn't very often, her smile made me feel like there was nothing wrong in the whole world, and I knew she loved me.

"Stay out of there, that's not for you kids," she'd bark if she caught us digging around in her "secret" candy drawer. If any of us were in the house alone with her, though, she'd let us pick out a treat. If anyone else saw us with the candy, Gram would act as if we had stolen it behind her back. Everyone was onto her games, but we always played along. She would travel to wherever we lived to visit us throughout the years before she passed away. Gram was the absolute best!

DYSFUNCTION

On the last day of our vacation, we went to a picnic at a local orphanage on the Philly side of the Delaware River because my Uncle Joe had some kind of connection there. Mom told us that our Jersey family didn't care for crossing the bridge, joking that Philadelphia was too rough for them, but they all came over that day. Uncle Joe dressed up like a tiger for the kids, and everyone had fun. The picnic was a good way for all of us to say goodbye before we headed back to Louisiana the next day. I was looking forward to going home.

I went down by the riverbank, thinking about what I was going to do first when I got home and who I wanted to see. I missed my friends. As I looked back up toward the picnic, I saw my parents heading down toward me. They stood there with me, making small talk about the trip and seeing our relatives, then my dad blurted out, "We're not going back, kid."

I just stared at them. I couldn't believe it. I didn't want to believe it. I had friends, I had a boyfriend, I had a life! I felt a combination of sadness and anger starting to grow, and I defiantly fought back the tears at the thought of once again losing everything.

"Your grandparents aren't doing well, and we want to stay here to be close to them," Mom added. The thoughts in my head were coming fast and furious. *My grandparents seemed just fine. They must have had this planned all along. What a dirty trick they played on us.* I walked away from them without a word, confident that the look on my face sufficiently expressed my disapproval.

Dad was leaving the next day to go back down to Louisiana on his own to get our things. Whatever could fit in one vehicle, just like all the other times. I begged to go with him so I could say goodbye and get my important items.

"No, just give me a list of the things you want."

A list of the things I want … how about everything that is mine! I called him while he was down there, desperate to remind him of my list. That was a long-distance call, and I was told not to call again.

It didn't take us long to go through the car when Dad got back. Frantically searching for whatever belonged to me, I quickly realized that only a few items from my list had made it, but not my diaries. They were my refuge through everything. It crushed my heart to imagine Dad throwing piles of our personal belongings into a dumpster like they meant nothing, especially my diaries. I was outraged by their lack of respect for my feelings and what was important to me. I did not speak to my parents for months. My dad tried to console me, but Mom took her usual stance: "She'll get over it."

I wanted to be as far away from Mom and Dad as possible, but I was too young to get a job in Philadelphia. You had to be sixteen years old to get your working papers, and I was only fifteen, so I got a paper route and even volunteered to fill in for others who couldn't do their routes. That got me out of Gram's house where we were living and away from my parents for at least a few hours a day until I made some new friends to hang out with.

The four of us kids slept on cots in the front bedroom of Gram's house. My parents slept in the middle room. My great-grandmom would come in the room at the crack of dawn, grumbling under her breath as she opened the window shades, "If these kids think they are going to sleep all day, they have another thing coming to them." That was our cue to get up and get moving. We were not allowed to go downstairs in our pajamas. You had to be fully dressed and ready for whatever the adults needed you to do.

I started tenth grade at Abraham Lincoln High School, the same high school Mom attended back in the day. I joined the dance club, Future Business Leaders of America, the school newspaper, the drama club, and the flag drill team. I thoroughly enjoyed being on the dance team in our school play, *Oklahoma!* and even got to be an extra in *Rocky III* because Sylvester Stallone had gone to Lincoln. He invited the school to participate in the movie, so the band, color guard, majorettes, flag drill team, and some others got to be extras in the scene where Rocky gets a statue dedicated to him on the top of the Philadelphia Art Museum steps. The seniors got to be in the front row, and the rest of us gathered behind them. Since I was a sophomore, I was in the back, and you can see only the tip of my flag drill flag in the movie, but my family doesn't have any trouble making fun of me for my split-second starring role. They play the scene, rewind, play the scene again, and rewind to point out the tip of my flag. It's a long-standing joke and actually pretty funny.

Between tenth and eleventh grade, we moved out of Gram's house and into a rowhome about seven city blocks away. Debbie and I had to walk right by our great-grandmother's house on our way to and from school every day until we got a car. We were old enough to have jobs after school by then and didn't stop to say hello as much as we could have. Our whole family would see Gram in church on Sunday, though, and seeing her was always special.

Mom had gotten a job at a bank downtown and Dad took a job as the supervisor of a trucking company. They worked hard, became friends with some of the neighbors, and both started spending evenings away from the home. Dad would go out "drinking with the guys" every Friday night, which made Mom so mad that she'd put ipecac in the glass of milk he'd have when he got home from drinking to make him throw up. She was more obvious about what she was doing; she had guys pick her up right outside our front door. The constant fighting had calmed down while we were living in Gram's house, but now it was back in full force.

I met my first love on that new block. Michael lived a few houses down and across the street. You'd typically see a bunch of neighbors sitting out on their front steps on any given night. I'd sit out there like everyone else and glance down the street at Mike. He was a couple of years older than me — tall, dark, muscular, and devilishly handsome. When he smiled, his whole face lit up and his eyes twinkled. It didn't take long before I was head over heels for him.

NOT GOOD ENOUGH

Mike and I went to my Junior Prom together, and I became the Junior Prom Queen by having my prom ticket drawn from a box. I was very excited, and after the ceremonial flowers were given and pictures were taken for the yearbook, I found the nearest pay phone in the hall and called my mom.

"Mom, I was just crowned Junior Prom Queen," I shared with excitement when she answered the phone.

"How did they decide that?"

"They pulled tickets from a box."

"So, you didn't win based on anything besides them pulling your ticket?" I could hear the familiar sound of disappointment in her voice. "I guess that was lucky for you then," she added dismissively. "They didn't decide things like that when I was back in school."

As I became a teenager and began to develop physically, the dynamic between Mom and me felt like a competition. We had all heard the stories over the years of how she was a beauty queen, had guys falling all over her in school, went to lots of proms, got straight A's, and basically walked on water. I set out to do the same or better.

Dad was always supportive and proud of my accomplishments. Mom wanted more of his attention and didn't like that I got some of it. She still expected him to shower her with all his attention, despite how she treated him. My mom tried pitting us against each other in an attempt to break our bond. When that didn't work, she reverted to mistreating us both.

My relationship with Dad was easier for the most part. We'd be the only ones who woke up early. On Sunday mornings, we would drive around the corner to the gas station mini-mart and pick up a gallon of milk and the Sunday newspaper. Then we would go next door to Dunkin' Donuts and get two dozen donuts and a large coffee with extra cream and sugar for Mom. Back at home, everyone was still sleeping, and the house was quiet. We would get two glasses of milk, grab our favorite donuts, and read the paper together (Dad would give me the comics and the entertainment section). Those were some of my favorite moments with my dad.

Mom made fun of my shyness, the way I dressed, and my newfound love. She pushed my sisters and me to look pretty and was quick to point out when we didn't. She felt compelled to warn me against men by telling me things like they only care about themselves, they do whatever they want, they are stupid and easily led, they only want one thing, and they can't be trusted.

"The best advice I can give you about men is, get them before they get you," she'd say. Mom dressed provocatively and wore a lot of makeup. She made sure she looked good whenever she left the house, loving any attention she drew to herself. "These are power," she'd say as she reached under her large breasts and held them up. "Learn to use them."

My opinion of men had already been polluted by what happened to me six years earlier in the five-and-dime store, so I readily believed what she told me.

ANXIETY

I had my first panic attack at seventeen while Mike and I were in a casino in Atlantic City, New Jersey. I got into the casino by dressing sexy and piling on the makeup but had my older sister's ID with me if I needed it because the legal gambling age was eighteen in 1982. Mike was nineteen. While he was playing blackjack, I was wandering around the slot machines and drinking seven and sevens, but I hadn't eaten much that day. Suddenly, a wave of dread came over me and I felt dizzy. I began to hyperventilate and all I could think was that I had to get out of the casino immediately, or I was going to die. I started making my way to the exit but fainted by the door. Security took me to the casino's medical office and asked for my ID. I gave them my sister's name and told them who I was with and where they could find him in the casino. They found Mike and we headed home.

That first panic attack happened days after I lost my virginity. I was in love with Mike and felt I was ready. I asked my dad to take me to Planned Parenthood for birth control because Mom would not talk to me or my siblings about sex. Although she was a sexual person, she made me think sex was something dirty by the way she spoke about it in general. I suspect that was from her upbringing. My dad questioned my readiness and advised me to be careful if I was determined to proceed.

I didn't know much about how to have sex except for what I heard from girlfriends. Mike and I had gone to the Lincoln Drive-In a couple of times, where they showed X-rated movies. I heard horror stories about pain and bleeding the first time.

Debbie and Patrick were always out, and my parents would be out with my little sister Jennifer at a school function, so I planned my first time for that night. I took the sheets off my bed and wrapped the mattress in big, black trash bags. I made the bed again with an old sheet I could throw out without anyone knowing it was gone, fully anticipating a crime-scene-type experience. Although my first time was clumsy, it was also very gentle and sweet with someone I believed I loved very much. I felt safe with him, and we had fun. I also found out that all of that preparation was unnecessary.

I was not hurt or mistreated by Mike in any way, but the nightmares about being sexually abused returned. The anxiety felt like a life-or-death urgency to escape, which brought my nervous system back to those moments in the five-and-dime store and how I desperately wanted to leave. I never told my parents or Mike about the abuse and didn't tell Mom I was having sex. When I talked to her about the panic attack, she assumed my anxiety was caused by having too many activities on my plate.

"Yup, sounds like a panic attack. I've got something for the next time you have one," she said as she dug through her purse and pulled out a pill bottle. She opened the bottle and pulled out a tiny, white bar with three indents, dividing it into four sections. Each section was 0.25 mg of Xanax, and you could break off however many sections you needed to solve your issue.

I was at a beef and beer with friends when I had the next panic attack. I took a section of the pill Mom gave me, and it calmed me down. I was relieved to have something to dull the feeling that I was about to die.

ADDICTION

Mom had a pill for anything and everything. She took meds for anxiety, depression, pain, bowel problems, stomach issues, and a few other ailments. It seemed like she was popping them my entire life. She never took them as prescribed by the doctor, but in the doses she determined would give her the feeling she was looking for or take away the feeling she wanted to avoid. Two things were very important to my mom: her cigarettes and her pills. If you tried to take either away, she became a lunatic. She would cry and lash out in anger, displaying a roller coaster of emotions, saying the most awful things.

NOT GOOD ENOUGH

Between what I heard from my mother about men and Mike choosing to spend more time with his friends than me, I began to look elsewhere for the attention I needed. I cheated on him by going out with someone I worked with at McDonald's, and we broke up. I went to several proms, got good grades (especially in math, just like Mom), and made sure I kept the upper hand in my romantic relationships by having one foot out — meaning I never fully committed to anyone. I was always ready to run and "get them before they got me."

I was constantly on the go, attending school, working, and running around with friends and boyfriends. That pace landed me in the hospital toward the end of my senior year with walking pneumonia. I lost a lot of time in school, and my rank slipped. When I graduated from Lincoln High School in 1983, they called out the names of the top fifty students in our class of approximately six hundred and twenty-five. I knew my name was not going to be called. Mom could barely stand next to me or look at me when we were taking pictures after graduation. I could see the disgust on her face with her pursed lips and angry eyes. Her reaction reminded me of when I had finished second back in fifth grade. I disappointed her again, and she didn't talk to me for weeks. She never talked to me about her expectations but punished me for not living up to them.

After graduation, I started taking acting lessons and went to Barbizon Modeling School with my sister Jennifer. I wanted to be an actress and thought modeling would be a good way to learn how to be more attractive. Mom was adamant that my sisters and I take care of our appearance. It was a grueling schedule since I was working as a bookkeeper at an electrical service company and also taking some accounting courses at Philadelphia Community College at night. My acting teacher was John Barth, and he was eccentric. I think he felt he was more famous than he was and projected an inflated opinion of himself, but I enjoyed every minute of those classes in downtown Philadelphia.

For graduation from modeling school, we put on an impressive fashion show for our friends and families. There were four outfit changes ranging from casual to formal, and we each strutted our stuff down the runway to the top hits of 1984. All graduates were to give a speech after we performed, and most of the other students planned on thanking their parents for their support. I took a stand against my mother's judgment and didn't even mention her in my speech as I looked at her table. Instead, I thanked my boyfriend at the time, Joe, for being so supportive. He was sitting right next to her. She was furious, and I was happy not to talk to her for another couple of weeks.

I entered the Miss Pennsylvania pageant early the following year. I solicited local businesses for sponsorship to help pay for the outfits I needed and my travel expenses. The neighborhood newspaper, *The Northeast Times*, even sent a reporter to write a story about my adventure. My family was excited and helped me raise a little money for the trip. Mom even arranged for someone to lend me a Mummer's costume for the regional representation portion of the competition.

The pageant was being held five hours away in Greensburg, Pennsylvania. I was able to catch a ride out there with one of the other contestants. The first few days were full of interviews, smaller competitions, and practice for the main event, where the winner would be crowned. My parents and boyfriend Joe made the trip to see the finale that weekend and pick me up.

The final competition had four segments: swimsuit, casual dress, regional representation, and formal gown. I could see my parents in the audience as I walked the runway for each segment but couldn't gauge the blank stare on Mom's face. At the end of the formal gown segment, they announced the winner. I didn't look for my mom when my name was not called. I already knew what was coming. She didn't talk to me for the entire five-hour ride home and for a couple of weeks after. When you failed her, she acted like you didn't exist. My dad and the rest of my family were proud of me for the effort, and I enjoyed the entire experience of the competition.

Looking back, I understand that Mom couldn't see past her own disappointments to realize that I had entered the competition to get her attention and approval. Watching me trying to be like her and accomplish the same things she bragged about and was so proud of herself for only reminded her of her own shortcomings. My dad's support often caused tension between them, but I was grateful that he was willing to endure her anger and encourage me. She refused to give me any credit for all the hard work I put in and everything I had accomplished, which kept me stuck in the cycle of trying to do more for her approval.

AVOIDANCE

Someone I worked with at the electrical service company had a friend looking for a roommate, and I couldn't wait to move out of my parents' house. Mom was a bully, and most of the time I felt like a coward around her. I was petrified to tell her I was planning to move out, so I wrote a note.

"I'll miss you guys and thanks for helping me grow into the independent woman I've become," was some of the sucking up I included to soften the blow. I left the note on the dining room table where Mom usually put on her makeup, and I left the house quickly for the day thinking she would calm down after a few hours.

I stayed busy the entire day and headed home that night thinking she would've cooled down. When I got there, all of my stuff was in big, black trash bags out on the front steps.

"If you're leaving, you can just get out now," she said with that familiar look of disgust on her face. The place I was moving to was not ready, so I threw my bags in the blue Ford Pinto I had bought for $250 down on Kensington Avenue and stayed with some friends for a few days. I'm convinced she only let me come back so she could act like I did not exist by ignoring me.

Debbie was married and Patrick joined the Army. I felt bad about abandoning my little sister Jennifer, who was thirteen, leaving her alone there to deal with the drama between my parents. I was unaware of the debilitating beliefs stuck in my body by then: I'm unlovable, I'm a coward, life is a struggle, money is only for the privileged, no one cares how I feel, everyone is for sale, men are dangerous, relationships don't work, and no one can be trusted, including me. I headed off full of anxiety and free to start creating my own version of drama, which I did.

PART THREE

PACK YOUR BAGGAGE
FOR ADULTHOOD

Hurt people hurt people. That's how pain patterns get passed on, generation after generation after generation.

—Rabbi Yehuda Berg

MOVING OUT

After an explosion in a movie, with big chunks of debris flying through the air then falling to the ground, what remains is a cloud of dust that hovers and finally settles over everything. This is how I see my childhood, as an explosion of emotional pain that created layers of trauma dust that settled on every area of my life as an adult.

I had looked forward to the day I could move out of my parents' house. I thought all of my troubles would be over once I didn't have to worry about what I was going home to. There would be no rules, no pressure to please anyone, and no requirement to "keep the peace." I thought I would be free, and for a while I was, but chaos was my comfort zone, and I quickly returned to it.

DYSFUNCTION

My new roommate, Heather, was an interior designer who was almost ten years older than me. Her apartment was beautifully decorated in mauve and seafoam green with black lacquer accent furniture that was so popular in the eighties. We got along well but had different lifestyles because of our age difference. She was an established adult, and I was just getting started.

The apartment was about forty minutes away from my parents' house and over an hour away from my job. I found a new position with a construction company that was right up the street from the apartment and worked for them as a receptionist and assistant bookkeeper. I also continued to take accounting courses at Bucks County Community College at night.

Most of my friends were still living at home and going to college full-time to become lawyers, pharmacists, actuaries, and accountants, including my boyfriend, Joe. Our close-knit group did almost everything together. We rented houses down the shore in Sea Isle City, New Jersey, for the summers, went on skiing trips, rented cabins in the Poconos in the winter, and filled every weekend with some sort of party or adventure. I loved how smart and fun they all were.

My anxiety and panic attacks persisted, happening more frequently. The cycle in my family of origin was you hurt someone, they don't talk to you for a while, you start talking again for some random reason and act like nothing ever happened — never addressing anyone's wounds. Mom and I were back to pretending nothing bad ever happened between us, so she was willing to hook me up with some Xanax.

While planning one of my trips to see Mom for the meds, she mentioned that she was going to have a medical test done and would need help with an enema while I was there. I wasn't sure what that was at twenty-three, but I was willing to help Mom out. She had recently divorced my dad and was living in a small apartment with my younger sister. Jennifer was fifteen and, like the rest of us, never wanted to be home, so I asked her to be there to help me with Mom.

I arrived around the same time Jennifer was getting home and Mom explained to us that she needed to "clean out her bowels" for the medical test she was having the next day. It was 1988, long before cell phones and googling instructions on how to do things, so Mom proceeded to describe how enemas work. Jennifer was horrified at my mother's request and my expectation of her help.

I rummaged around Mom's apartment for a funnel to get the water inside her and a bucket to catch anything coming out of her. I took the ink out of a pen and attached a tinfoil cone to the end as the funnel, grabbed a cup to pour the water, and took a bucket from her broom closet. Mom undressed and leaned over the bathtub in her tiny bathroom. My mother is not a small woman, and the sight of her bare ass up in the air was quite disturbing.

"Jen, do you want to hold her butt cheeks open or pour the water in?" I asked, barely able to get the words out without laughing because Jennifer was already crying in disbelief, and I thought the entire thing was so absurd.

"I can't do this! Why are you making me do this?" Jennifer protested.

"Mom needs help. We have to help her."

"I'm not pouring the water in her!" Jennifer said as she reached in from the hallway, trying to stay as far away from what I was about to do as she could, and held my mother's cheeks open while I inserted the makeshift funnel into her bottom. "Hurry up and get it done Denise!"

I poured two cups of water into the funnel. Jennifer was crying and urging me to hurry up, and my mom started laughing, which made her start to fart the water back out of the tube I had inserted into her butt. I started screaming because water was shooting out all over the place. At that point, my older sister Debbie ran out of the bedroom and started taking pictures of the entire fiasco. Turns out, it was a practical joke my mother and older sister were playing on us. I was hysterical with laughter and Jennifer was raging mad.

When Debbie went to pick up the pictures after they were developed at the store, she got somebody else's baby shower pictures and they got her pictures. She promptly contacted the store, and sure enough the other people had already returned her pictures. I still have them.

I started moving around from place to place and even temporarily moved into that tiny apartment with Mom and Jennifer. My friends called me "The Bag Lady" because I never stayed in one place long enough to unpack my stuff from the big black trash bags that I lived out of.

From remembering the messages I heard during the molestation, watching Mom blatantly cheat for years while Dad cheated on the down-low, listening to Mom trash-talk her exes, and remembering her advice "to get them before they get you," I had little respect for most men. None of them felt safe to me. My appearance became an asset, though, just like Mom said. The attention I received from a growing number of the opposite sex became like a drug, and I got hooked. Finally, I began to feel wanted. I knew in the back of my mind though that the attention came with expectations. My self-respect was so low that I was willing to take that deal, but only as long as I was in control of it, choosing who I wanted. I got the adoration and approval I craved after a childhood without it, and they got sex with a pretty girl. If they got attached, I got out.

Joe and I had been dating for several years, since high school. He had asked me to marry him on my twenty-third birthday, and we planned to be married the following year. The gowns and tuxes were ordered, the hall was booked, we took Pre-Cana classes and made promises to the Catholic Church. Our friends were lined up to be in the wedding party, we even bought a house together, and still, I couldn't go through with it. I was already cheating on him and wound up calling off our wedding only a few months before our wedding day.

Joe deserved better than me. He was one of the nicest guys I've ever known. All I could see in my mind was a marriage full of lies like my parents had — a marriage I didn't want. In keeping with my pattern of avoidance, I wrote Joe a letter, hopped on a plane to Florida to stay with the Stajkowski side of my family, and had my sister Debbie call everyone to tell them the wedding was off. I broke Joe's heart and lost most of my friends in the process.

After that, I continued to date the person I was cheating on Joe with and eventually fell in love. Craig was much older than me with a full and successful adult life — exciting to a twenty-four-year-old. We had a lot of fun, traveled, partied, and talked about our future together. I wanted to marry him, but he was a cheater too. I was naive to think our love was enough to stop him from all the deception just because I was willing to stop — it wasn't. Our relationship ended with him shoving me out of a window and another woman he was involved with dragging me by my hair into an epic three-way confrontation with him. I was hysterical when I left his place and drove to the closest pay phone to call my sister Jennifer, hoping that she would tell me everything would work out for Craig and me. Instead, she bid him good riddance.

The pain of our childhood showed up more harshly in my little sister. She doesn't take any shit from anyone, and she's been trying to teach me to do the same for a long time. Later, I began to think that my relationship and heartbreak with Craig was karmic payback for what I had done to Joe. I certainly deserved it.

I went on a dating binge. Just like with Mom, no one was off limits. "Why settle for a copy when you can have the original," she used to say when she would hit on some of my boyfriends. A couple of the men I saw were married. Those acquaintances were safer for me because I knew they weren't looking for a relationship, and neither was I. If I dated anyone who turned out to be "too nice," I'd sabotage the whole thing and move on, thinking I did not deserve them and that I would only cause them pain. I kept my heart closed to the risks of developing feelings for anyone. I felt that I couldn't trust or be trusted.

AVOIDANCE

I was twenty-four years old and constantly on the move in one way or another — men, addresses, friends, jobs, businesses, classes, drinking, having fun. I even tried a couple of illicit drugs, wondering if they really could help me escape myself, but the thought of turning into a drug addict, like I perceived my mother to be, frightened me. It was a vicious cycle of avoiding my feelings of unworthiness, wanting more, and trying to be better, but nothing was good enough, just like me — not good enough.

Chasing more money and the arbitrary circumstances that I thought would make me happy filled my focus. I joined multi-level marketing organizations to get rich, became a real estate agent to flip houses, took tax processing classes to make more money, started a small business selling gift baskets and silk flower arrangements to gain freedom, tried out for the Philadelphia Eagles Cheerleaders to get attention, and attended several self-help retreats to find out what was wrong with me. I was trying to control the dissatisfaction in my life, but the harder I tried, the more out of control it felt. I was frustrated that I couldn't figure out what I wanted. Seeking happiness felt like clumsily grasping for a balloon that unraveled its tie from my wrist, floating further and further away.

FEAR

As my anxiety continued to worsen, I did not want to go through the interrogation that came with getting more Xanax from Mom, so I decided to see a therapist. I wanted to talk about my childhood, my lack of conviction that any relationship could work, my relentless pursuit of my mother's approval, my love-hate relationship with money, and most importantly, the sexual abuse I suffered at ten. All the things I had never talked about with anyone.

I specifically chose a woman therapist thinking she would be more understanding. I would show up at her office with a pen and notebook, ready to take copious notes about why I was messed up and her suggestions on how I could get better. I expected the therapist to "fix" me. At twenty-four years old, I thought that's what therapists did. Conversely, she made me feel worse. She explained that deep down, I believed that something in me must be sacrificed to get money. She had me write my name on a large piece of paper, then stand on it to represent what a "doormat" I was for my mother and in my relationships. Then she told me that a high number of abused people become abusers themselves in the same way. That idea filled me with fear. I had learned not to trust people throughout my childhood, but now I was afraid I couldn't trust myself either.

THE AMERICAN DREAM

When I got pregnant unexpectedly at twenty-seven, I was petrified. I was single and living with my brother in a rowhome in Philadelphia. I thought that the self-help books I was reading had helped me become a better person in some ways, but I wasn't sure I could be a good mother. *I want to be the mother I wish I had.* The fear of damaging my child like my parents had damaged me consumed me.

I thought back to the day I was sitting in the cafeteria of Fox Chase Hospital, in the last few hours of my grandmother's life, with Mom, a couple of her sisters, and my older sister Debbie. They were talking about how they thought my grandfather was mishandling the situation, and sharing some of their own dysfunctional history from their upbringing.

"Don't take the dysfunction of our family into your own families," my Aunt Linda warned. Now that I was about to become a mom, I felt the pressure of my aunt's advice.

My baby's father, Gary, and I had only been seeing each other casually for a very short time. We both worked for the same general contractor; he was a project manager, and I was a bookkeeper. We got to know each other while playing tennis with our coworkers a couple of nights a week after work. Gary had wavy, dark brown hair and a moustache. He was smart, cute, funny, and could fix a broken shelf and repair my car. He'd pack me lunch and bring it into the office with sweet little love notes inside. Although we had fun together, most of what we connected on was the trauma from our childhoods — not a very good foundation. We loved each other in the ways we were capable of at the time, but neither of us had any good relationship role models. Still, we decided to try and make our impending family work.

Our son was born via C-section after I had pushed for eight hours. Gary was with me through the entire process. It was after 11:00 p.m. when I got back to my hospital room. Gary left with my mother's boyfriend, Ted, who was a little younger than me, and Mom sat with me for a few moments before leaving herself.

She came back to the hospital in the morning, but we didn't see Gary or Ted until later that afternoon, both hungover from being out together the night before. By then, my mom had convinced me to name my son Gary Jr., even though I wanted to name him Eric the entire time I was pregnant. She also tried to convince me that breastfeeding was dirty, and I shouldn't do it.

Giving birth, going through surgery, having my mother in my ear, and having another human being to take care of were very overwhelming. On top of that, my brother Patrick had to take off work to pick the baby and me up from the hospital and bring us back to his house where I was living. It hurt me that Gary Sr. would not take the day off to bring us home.

The bedroom I occupied in the house my brother rented had a bed, a bureau, and now the cradle that my grandfather made many years before that had held a couple of my younger aunts and uncle, my older sister Debbie's kids, and now held my firstborn.

My brother and his wife had just had their first child a few months earlier, and the house was not big enough for all of us, so I moved in with Mom and her boyfriend, Ted. Their apartment was closer to my job at the general contractor and to where Gary Sr. was living with his mother in Yardley. Mom was willing to babysit Little Gary while I worked.

DYSFUNCTION

Several months later, I had saved enough money to buy a row-home on my own in Northeast Philadelphia so that my new family, which consisted of Big Gary, Little Gary, and me, could live the American dream under the same roof. I was proud of myself because it looked like my life was becoming more "normal." I was in a committed relationship, had a beautiful baby boy, and now owned a home where I could do things differently than my parents. Proof that my heart could love showed in my intense feelings for my baby boy, and I had the highest hopes for the success of my new family.

I started a new job as a bookkeeper in Center City, Philadelphia, continued selling real estate, and enrolled Little Gary in a local daycare facility. Dropping him off early each morning before I went to work was heartbreaking.

Instead of being happy for me, Mom took me to court for the rent she was losing because of my moving out. Being served court papers and sitting in a courtroom in front of a judge, accused by my mother of running out on my responsibilities, was humiliating. The judge dismissed the case because my name was not on the lease.

I was trying to improve my life and to provide my son a home with both of his parents. I honestly did not know what I had done that was so wrong that my mother would go to those lengths to hurt me. I broke down and sobbed uncontrollably as I walked outside the courtroom doors. Mom tried to approach me outside, apologizing as she walked toward me. I just walked away.

Caring for a baby requires a new set of skills that aren't automatically downloaded when you give birth. Becoming a mom for the first time reminded me of what the therapist had told me, that the abused may become abusers in the same way. I considered my abuser a child sexual predator. That made me question everything I did with Little Gary. When I tried to breastfeed, I remembered my mother telling me it was perverted, which made me feel like I was doing something inappropriate, so I stopped. The innocent act of giving my son his baths had me overly aware of every move I made. The sexual abuse I endured as a child was affecting my experience of mothering, and I brought shame to the most basic tasks. I was filled with guilt and sadness. I used to silently say, "I'm sorry," to Little Gary as I held him in my arms and hoped he wouldn't feel my anxieties. I hoped he could feel that he was loved.

I never felt comfortable enough to discuss how I was feeling with Big Gary. Depression set in, and I started to eat my way through the uneasiness. I'm not sure if I was experiencing post-partum depression, but the comfort of chaos returned. Big Gary and I began a cycle of breaking up and making up, moving in and moving out, and in all those comings and goings, we had another son together, Steve.

I was thirty-two when I had Steve. We were living in Lang-horne in a single-family foreclosure property we wanted to flip. Big Gary was with me for Steve's birth, as was my sister Debbie — who I chose to be in the delivery room over my mother. I pushed for a couple of hours before they took me to surgery for an emergency C-section.

That birth took a lot out of me. I developed an infection and had to stay in the hospital for several days. My mother never came to see me or the baby because I had chosen to have Debbie in the delivery room instead of her. Once again, I had to find my own ride home from the hospital and called Big Gary's mother to pick us up.

In the four years after Little Gary was born, I found my way and began to trust myself as a mother. I was gentle, caring, and completely in tune with Little Gary and Steve's needs. I could see that my sons were safe and happy, making me confident that I was never a threat to my children like the therapist had suggested I might be.

Big Gary and I desperately wanted to figure out our relationship so we could keep the family together, but we both had unresolved personal issues. Ironically, he accused me of cheating on him ad nauseam. He refused to believe I was out actually trying to improve our lives by taking night classes or going to self-improvement seminars. He expected me to be home taking care of the boys, and his accusatory tone got old.

I expected Big Gary to be home more, working on his relationships within our family instead of out partying with his friends so much. We also disagreed on parenting styles and how the boys should be raised.

9

WHY CAN'T I GET THIS RIGHT?

Shortly before Big Gary and I split the first time, I broke my foot. Little Gary was four and Steve was six months. I worked as a property manager, and I took both of them to work with me each day. Wearing a cast up to my knee, I would pack the car, drive us into the office, load Steve into the stroller, put the portable crib on the top of the stroller, drape the diaper bag and cooler that held snacks and bottles on the sides of the stroller, grab Gary by the hand and hobble my way into the office building to a suite on the top floor. I would set up one of the empty offices like a daycare and hope that the boys were not too much of a distraction for my boss. Each day was a battle against the clock and my sanity.

When the house in Langhorne sold, the boys and I moved in with my sister Debbie for a few months before I bought another rowhome in Philadelphia. Debbie would watch the boys for me while I went to work. My brother Patrick came to live with me for a while after his marriage ended. A year later, the boys and I moved back in with Big Gary.

ANXIETY

The second time we split, Little Gary was six and Steve was two. Throughout my "on again, off again" relationship with their dad, I was a single mother, and trying to keep it all together overwhelmed me. The three of us lived in a small apartment. I would wake up at the crack of dawn, get ready for my full-time job, get them prepared for school and daycare, drop them off as early as I could, and race to get to work on time (an hour's drive in traffic). I would work my eight hours and not a minute longer — I had to race home to pick them up at day-care before closing so that I wouldn't be charged a late fee I couldn't afford. I would make dinner, get them to T-ball, then baths and bedtime stories. Those were the days everything went right — throw in sicknesses, injuries, weather, and car trouble, and those days felt like I had to climb Mount Everest. By the time I sat down at night after laundry, bills, dishes, and cleanup, it was almost time to get up and do it all again.

There was only one night, in all of my life's madness, that I thought, *I don't care if I wake up tomorrow*. I was exhausted. I couldn't do it anymore. I could see the similarities with my own childhood, and I felt like I was doing everything wrong. My worst fears were coming true: I was making choices that could mess up my children. I was at the point where I thought they'd be better off without me.

I slept on the couch by the front door in case anyone tried to break in. When I finally fell asleep that night, I dreamt I was floating above my body, looking down at myself sleeping on the couch. In my dream, I watched a bright, white light surround me as I lay there and then saw myself back in my body on the couch, still surrounded by the bright light, and a circle of roses began to spin right above me.

When I woke up, the load seemed lighter, and my strength was renewed. It had been a long time since I had the energy to go to church, but I felt that dream was my reminder from God that he is always with me. I could run from everything else in my life, but I was not going to run from my responsibilities as a mother, even if I felt like I was failing.

DYSFUNCTION

There would be one more move back in with Big Gary before we finally called it quits. I wanted to give it one last try for the boys but probably should have known better by then. The gap between our expectations of each other and the relationship was too big. The lack of trust we both felt crushed any chance of survival.

The boys and I moved to an apartment in Norristown that was further from family, but much closer to my job in Plymouth Meeting. I was working for an IT consulting company as an assistant controller. Mom moved in with me to help with the boys. She had taken turns living with each one of her children throughout the years. This was the fifth time I'd lived with her since I couldn't wait to move out of my parents' house.

One day, I came home from work, and she had the boys loosely tied to two dining room chairs with signs around their necks. One said, "I'm Bad," and the other said, "I Don't Listen." I should've thrown her out then, but I was still blinded by my obsession for her approval and love. Seeing them reminded me of a story Debbie told me about Mom tying us up when we were very small. Gary and Steve pulled the strings off easily and laughed it off. I apologized to the boys for their grandmother's behavior and explained to them that it was her idea of a joke.

"Don't ever do that again!" I warned her in a tone of anger.

In 2001, online dating was just getting popular. My friend Margie would help me weed through the profiles each week, and she and our other friend Mae, along with their husbands, would show up at the restaurants where I was having dinner on my first dates. They would sit at another table to keep an eye on me in case I needed to be rescued.

After the events of 9/11 happened, I noticed a change in the way people viewed their lives and relationships. The need for connection felt more intense on the dating scene. In less than a year, I met someone online who had long-term potential. Harvey had salt and pepper hair, a goofy but sweet smile, and a silly sense of humor. He shared that he was at the top of his class during his time in the army and was currently climbing the ladder in his IT career. My company was bought by a larger corporation, and I started doing some consulting. Harvey and I would spend hours talking on the phone some nights after the boys went to bed. We started dating and had fun trying new things with the boys, like cutting down a Christmas tree and hiking through Valley Forge Park on the weekends.

We had been together for five months when we bought a house, got engaged, and moved in together, including my mother, who continued to babysit the boys. I felt as if I owed her a place to live since she had been helping me with my sons. We got married a few months later, and a year after that welcomed our son Christopher. It all happened so quickly, without enough discussion about our individual expectations of the relationship and our views on parenting. The tragedy of 9/11 exacerbated the need to create something meaningful in our lives. But I still showed up with my issues, and he showed up with his.

From the start, the marriage was difficult for both of us, and having my mother underfoot certainly did not help. Harvey struggled to fit into our well-established family dynamic, and I had a hard time with his inflexible opinions on how to run a household. Although Mom was there to watch the boys while we worked, she clashed with Harvey because they were a lot alike. After several tension-filled months, I gave my mother my minivan and helped her move into her own apartment.

I was laid off from my job around the time Christopher was born, and Harvey and I agreed that it would be good for all of us if I stayed home for a while with the kids instead of finding another job. I enjoyed those years being home to watch their growth, attend school field trips, volunteer, help with Scouts, go to practices, and just be a kid alongside them sometimes.

Losing half our income when I chose to stay home was financially tough. I handled the finances and didn't want Harvey to worry, so I was constantly looking for ways to cut corners or to make some money on the side. I tried some home distributor businesses but wasn't very good at that, so I got out. I wanted the boys to have everything I hadn't had, and that became harder.

In 2006, we moved to a smaller house to save some money. It was a four-bedroom colonial-style house in a great neighborhood, in a good school district. The boys each had their own room. We finished the basement for extra space for the kids and put a pool up in the backyard.

ANGER

Harvey was the main breadwinner and disciplinarian. Our parenting styles were the most significant conflict in our home. I did not agree with the military "break them down, then build them up" philosophy and the old "this is my house, and you'll do it my way" school of parenting that Harvey imposed on the boys (and sometimes tried to impose on me). He did not agree with my "let them be who they want to be" and "let them be heard" attitude. Being shut down as a kid made me want to offer my kids something different. I wanted them to know who they were. That what they thought and felt mattered to me. It was a battle of the wills, and I sold out my ideals at times to keep the peace. Our parenting was contradictory and confusing, but I would not argue in front of the kids if it could be avoided. I did not want them to develop the same anxieties I had around anger.

NOT GOOD ENOUGH

The sheer number of arguments we had over my son Gary having long hair, for example, was ridiculous. Harvey and Big Gary both put so much pressure on Gary to conform. I felt like I could not stop the "not good enough" cycle he was living in. Steve and Chris adjusted their behavior to avoid the same judgment. The oppression in our home was just like I'd experienced with my mother.

The children's fathers tried to change them into their version of what was acceptable. I fought to allow them to develop into who they are and to decide on certain things for themselves. I'm not saying that there shouldn't be rules for kids to follow to keep them safe, but personal autonomy regarding the length of his hair was a choice I thought Gary could handle as a teenager.

Little Gary came across as defiant, just like my older sister Debbie. I could see his struggle with trying to be himself while wanting the approval of Big Gary and his stepfather Harvey, and the self-destructive ways it showed up for him. My middle son, Steve, did what I did — people pleasing and staying busy to avoid the chaos, all while keeping up the outward impression that everything was fine. My youngest son, Chris, like my brother Patrick, remained invisible so as to not draw any negative attention to himself, working through his anxieties with humor and hiding his sadness. It all looked very familiar to me, and I felt like I was failing all of them.

I was trying to make my marriage work and to raise my boys differently than I had been raised. The pressure I put on myself to try and keep everyone happy was intense, and I was miserable. In retrospect, I realize that Gary's long hair wasn't the real issue at all; it was a combination of all the issues we disagreed on. The inability to communicate effectively and to solve our personal problems created frustration in everyone.

ADDICTION

After moving my mother into her own place, her addiction to prescription drugs intensified and her depression seemed worse. I decided to move her to a new apartment closer to where I lived so that I could watch over her. She was sixty-two years old and had had many falls, breakdowns, suicide attempts, and irrational behaviors over the years. Messages from the fall-alert people would come across my phone at all hours of the day and night.

I usually called my mom every day to check on her, but on the last day in March of 2007, there was no answer when I called before going out with friends. I figured she was napping as she did throughout her days, and I would try again in the morning.

The next day, I had a morning appointment at the local college to discuss taking some new classes. I planned to stop and see her after the meeting. I tried to call her again on my way to the college, but there was still no answer. Knowing her routines so well, a sick feeling began to bubble in my stomach, and I headed to her apartment instead. She lived in an old elementary school that had been turned into apartments for the elderly. You needed a code to enter the building and a key to enter each apartment. She had misplaced her key the week before, so I had temporarily given her mine. When I got there, her door was locked. I knocked several times — there was no answer. I felt a sense of dread, and I began to shake. I rushed to the front office, and they called the maintenance guy to let me in. I was terrified at the thought of what I was about to find inside her apartment.

As the door opened, I saw my mother lying on the floor near the door with her face in a pile of vomit. Her nightgown was pulled up at her waist, she had nothing on from the waist down, and she was lying in a puddle of urine. I froze.

The maintenance guy immediately began to shake her while calling her name, but she still did not move. I fell to the floor in the doorway, screaming "Mom" over and over to try and get a response. A few neighbors came out of their apartments to find out what the commotion was and moved me into the hallway as they called 911. I was hysterical and frantically asking if she was alive.

It didn't take long for the ambulance to arrive. The hospital was only five minutes away. The EMTs worked on her for a while and were able to revive her before moving her to the ambulance, but they would not let me ride along. I was so distraught that one of the neighbors had to drive me.

I had been to the hospital many times before with my mother, so my name was in their records as her emergency contact, power of attorney, and next of kin. It seemed like forever before they let me go to her room in the ER. When I got back there, I was greeted by a frenzy of activity. The nurse explained that Mom needed to be revived again in the ambulance. She was foaming at the mouth, one side of her face was blood red, and her left arm was swollen to three times its normal size. She was unconscious.

They took me to a separate, empty room and told me to call my family because my mother might not make it. I don't remember any of those conversations, but my sisters came up quickly and the three of us looked on as the medical team continued to work on Mom. Jennifer and I were beside ourselves with worry, holding on to every piece of information the staff shared like a lifeline. Debbie was angry because, once again, Mom was causing yet another high drama — she was the most levelheaded in the moment.

The ER team stabilized Mom and moved her to the ICU. They estimated that she had been lying on the floor for over twelve hours with her left arm caught under her body, cutting off the circulation and causing it to swell. Doctors were trying to save her arm but wanted my permission to amputate it if necessary. My mom is left-handed and the thought of her losing her dominant arm with my permission made me feel sick.

She had aspirated vomit into her lungs, and there was a threat of her developing pneumonia. The blood in her face had pooled on one side from the position she had lain in for so long. We were told that the following twenty-four hours of care would be critical to saving her arm and her life.

The next morning, when I could get in to see her, she was restrained. Her arms were strapped to the bedrails and her feet were strapped to the legs of the bed. Her face was swollen and bruised. The nurse told me that when she came out of the overdose, she had become combative. She was hostile and demanded to leave. The staff informed her that she would be staying; obviously she was not of a sound mind to make those decisions for herself. She proceeded to shout obscenities and to tell us all off while trying to break loose. It hurt me to see her in such a volatile state.

Mom spent thirty-four days in the hospital. They moved her from the ICU to a regular room and then to the psych ward. Her left arm responded to treatment and did not have to be amputated, although there was significant damage. Her fingers are stuck in a sort of bent claw, leaving her unable to firmly grip anything, and she has no strength in that arm anymore. She is permanently disabled.

For the next year and a half, I saw my mother almost every day, sometimes twice a day. I took her to every doctor's appointment, physical therapy appointment, and counseling session. I paid her bills, cleaned her apartment, shopped, did her laundry, modified her apartment for easier use of her left arm, set up home health aides and food deliveries, monitored her medications, and filled a locked pill machine each week that dispensed the correct dose of her meds twice a day.

I tracked her progress and her medications so that I could push her doctors to decrease them, and I was able to keep her from smoking. I had her eating better, and she lost weight. I also controlled her money, so her bank account increased. She was in the best physical, emotional, and financial shape she'd been in for years. The results of my dedication to her recovery made me very happy. The entire family was thrilled that she was doing so well.

DYSFUNCTION

One day, while I was over, Mom told me she wanted control of everything back: her bank account, her meds, her smoking, her life. She berated me when I tried to talk her out of it, so I gave it all back. The progress she had made in a year and a half, and all the time I spent getting her there, was undone in a matter of weeks. She went right back to the destructive habits that caused her overdose, and I was heartbroken.

I went back to receiving alerts that she had fallen and calls from the hospital when she had been brought into the ER, cleaning up after her, and being the person everyone called when there was a problem.

ANGER

I started working in accounting again and moved around to different jobs as I became bored. As soon as I stopped learning something new or felt the company was holding me back in some way, I moved on. Working and the responsibility of taking care of my mother distracted me from the turmoil happening at home. I thought that if we provided the kids with every "material" thing they needed or wanted, they would be content and spared from the same embarrassment I felt as a child. Harvey and I disagreed on almost everything and had given up on talking about our differences. In 2014, we separated for a year with the intention of working on our problems in counseling and figuring out if we could make the marriage work.

I moved out of our house and into a three-bedroom twin in the center of Boyertown. I thought I should be the one to move since I was the one who asked for the separation, and I felt guilty about that. Harvey asked me to reconsider the move, but I was convinced we needed the distance. There was a room for Chris, a room for me, and Gary and Steve shared a room. I intended for all the boys to come with me, but Christopher decided to spend most of his time at home with his dad. That made me regret my decision every day. I didn't realize how hard the separation was for him at eleven years old. I also didn't know how disruptive the separation would be to Steve's senior year in high school, but I saw that it was. He was angry and spent most of his time out partying with his friends. I didn't know how to help him through it.

Harvey and I went to counseling as planned, and we worked on our issues separately in a way that felt comfortable to each of us. I saw his efforts as a positive sign that he wanted to stay in the marriage, or maybe that's what I wanted to see. I judged my own selfishness and regretted the effects that had on my entire family.

In 2015, when the kids were twenty-two, eighteen, and twelve, we got back together. Gary, Steve, and I returned to the house with Harvey and Chris. Harvey and I had love for each other and our family, and there certainly were some good times, but it was apparent that we mostly just went through the motions. We spent most of our time doing our own things instead of spending time together. We tried to stay out of each other's way and remained cordial, but something was missing. Neither of us was willing to give up our positions on what we disagreed about, and our lack of communication got worse.

The Cosby trial had shaken my internal beliefs and stirred my discontent. In December of 2018, Harvey and I hosted a Christmas party for my side of the family, as we had done many times before. Everyone was drinking, having fun, playing games, and voting on who had the ugliest Christmas sweater. My dad, Pop-Pop Lou, won. The party was in full swing, and Harvey started to clean up as if the party was over. He was drunk and just wanted my family to leave. Jennifer and my niece were sitting at the island in our kitchen when I went in to ask him why he was cleaning up. He grabbed a butcher knife and waived it in my face, putting it to my throat saying, "I'm tired of your shit." He laughed like what he was doing was funny (he often played around with the knives in our kitchen). My niece yelled, and my sister froze. I stood my ground and just stared at him until he laughingly backed down. I'm not sure if I was angrier at his irresponsible display of humor or at the possibility of his joke getting out of hand, but I was tired of being bullied and tired of being the butt of his jokes. The scenario could've ended horribly. That's when I knew I was ready to leave the relationship for good.

I asked Harvey for a divorce in October of 2019 and moved out in December. Leaving my marriage was much more painful than I ever imagined it would be. But I'm confident it was necessary for both of us to find happiness in our lives.

TRUTH?

It became clear that my issues couldn't be resolved by swapping out the people in my life, changing where I lived, or altering any of my external circumstances. Harvey often called me the "common denominator" in our arguments about the boys. Within my own context, I could see how that was true. I was the common denominator in all of my life's struggles, and I accepted that there was work I had to do. I was determined to end the cycle, one way or another. I wanted to understand why I continued to sabotage my happiness. I was finally willing to unravel the brutal truths about myself and my story.

PART FOUR

TIME TO HEAL

The best way out is always through.

—Robert Frost

DONE WITH CRAZY

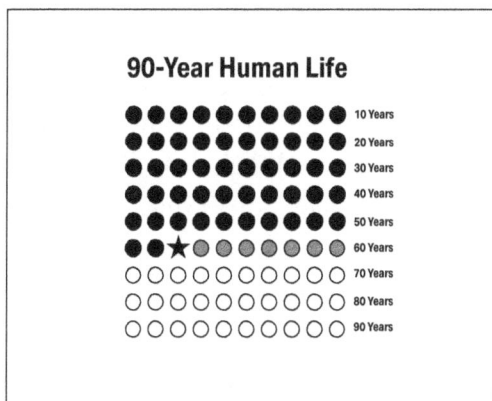

90-Year Human Life

(10 Years, 20 Years, 30 Years, 40 Years, 50 Years, 60 Years, 70 Years, 80 Years, 90 Years)

I was fifty-three years old in 2018 when I took the picture on the front cover and started my healing journey. I have just filled in the sixtieth space, which will account for two-thirds of my life, assuming I live to be ninety years old. Graphs similar to the one I've created here were poignant visual reminders that I did not have any more time to avoid the pain of my past. Even more upsetting than all the solid-filled dots that represent life lived was the fact that there are no guarantees of the count or quality of the blank dots that are left.

The first time I reflected on my entire past, I got mad as hell. In the weeks following the verdict of the Cosby trial in 2018, I spent my nights holed up in my home office, scribbling down thoughts in my journal. Fighting against the feelings of insignificance that were ingrained in me since childhood. I had every right to be angry about it. I was mad at my parents and my partners, but mostly mad at myself for doing exactly what my Aunt Linda had warned me about so many years before. I had brought the generational dysfunction of my family of origin into the family I created.

The implications of identifying as "not good enough" and the experiences I had in childhood planted the seed that I was "damaged." I had relied on self-help books and seminars to help me make sense of my unworthiness since I was a teenager, but I was still chasing some elusive form of approval. My parenting and relationships suffered as I continued to beat myself up over past mistakes. I had eaten my way through my anxieties, resulting in a five-foot, two-inch, two-hundred-pound woman full of judgment. I grew angrier every day while playing a character that had it all together.

Most of the changes I made throughout the years had been to my external circumstances: jobs, friends, relationships, locations, money, habits, and goals. I was beginning to think that the effort I had put into improving things hadn't made any difference at all. I had perpetuated constant change on the outside to avoid facing the pain buried deep down inside. Hidden wounds interfered with my ability to be happy.

Who am I? What do I want? What do I do next? Finding the answers to these questions became an obsession. Instead of listening to my protective character's vision of what was acceptable to others, I started listening to what my soul was screaming. The false beliefs I had developed through the years were disrupting my attempts to improve my life. I could see that it was time to concentrate solely on me, without considering what anyone else wanted or thought. It was time to take my life back!

As I continued to dredge up my past, my quest for the truth intensified. *Who was my biological father? Why did we move around so much? Why did my parents cheat? Why did they stay together so long? Why wasn't anything I did ever good enough for my mother?* I thought that having the answers might offer insight into what I believed about my childhood and myself. It was time to start talking.

I asked my mother some questions about the man she said was my biological father so that I could try to find him online. Robert Witherow from New Jersey was what she gave me. I took a DNA test through Ancestry, in hopes of matching with him or some relative of his.

Years before, I had found my brother's biological father, Bill McLeester, for his thirtieth birthday. Back then there was no internet or Google search available. I had to go to New Jersey and get a physical copy of the white pages in the telephone book from the area his family lived in when my mother knew him. Then I proceeded to call everyone that was listed with that last name, until I found his daughter. It turned out that they knew about Patrick and had been looking for him as well. I was ecstatic that I was able to do that for my brother. At the time, I didn't feel the need to find my own biological father because I considered my stepdad Lou to be my dad.

I went with Patrick to meet his father, Bill McLeester, and they were surprisingly similar for two people who had never spent time together. Patrick had his gestures, sense of humor, and smile. They had a few years together before Bill died, and I was happy that Patrick at least had that.

I asked Dennis Stajkowski, my older sister's father, if he knew all along that I wasn't his and about the other stories Mom had told me about him. Dennis apologized that he did not have more information about my biological father other than that he was a construction worker at a job site next to the diner my mom worked in at the time. He gave me copies of their divorce papers, showing that he had divorced Mom for adultery. Dennis also had papers showing he had paid child support until we started moving around so much that the checks couldn't find us. He even hired a private detective to find us at one point but had no luck. Learning that the stories Mom had told Debbie and me about Dennis were untrue fueled my growing anger.

I found out through an internet obituary that the man Mom said was my biological father had died. I was heartbroken that I would never meet him like my brother got to meet his father. Then, the DNA results came in. At fifty-four years old, I finally received confirmation that Dennis Stajkowski was a 99% match as my father.

"Hi Dennis, it's Denise," I said as my dad answered.

"Hi, how are you?" His voice was excited but faint. He had been battling an illness and sounded weak.

"Did you see the results of my DNA test come up on your Ancestry account?"

"Yes, I did, and I am very happy that we all have the truth now."

"Me too! I'm so sorry that everything happened the way it did. Thank you for answering all of my questions." I fought back tears of happiness and relief. "Well, I won't hold you up. We can chat more when you're feeling better."

"Oh, okay, I'll talk to you soon then. We have some catching up to do. Love you."

"Love you too Dad. Bye-bye."

The news was bittersweet for both of us. We had lost a lot of time together as father and daughter. It was a relief to finally know the truth about where I came from — for all those years, I had thought I was the unwanted, illegitimate result of an affair.

Mom looked genuinely surprised when I gave her the news about Dennis. "How about that" was her response, as if that giant puzzle piece of my life didn't matter. She even suggested the results were wrong. Although I wanted to bring up the discrepancies in her stories about Dennis, I knew it would be pointless. Mom always stuck to her story, no matter what proof you had to the contrary, and I wasn't willing to put myself through the aggravation.

As she drew in another long puff of her third cigarette, I asked her why she was so hard on me and why nothing I ever did was good enough. She looked at me as if I was exhausting her with my questions and dismissively said, "Because I always thought you could do better."

A few of my other questions went unanswered, meaning I couldn't really get a straight answer out of either of my parents, especially about why we moved around so much and why they had so many money problems. I may never know all the reasons why they behaved the way they did, but that would not stop me from moving forward with my own healing process.

The COVID pandemic hit a few months after I left my marriage. I had moved to a small two-bedroom apartment hoping Chris would come with me, but I understood why he remained in the house with his dad. That was the house he grew up in, and he had a lot more room for his belongings and for his life. Gary and Steve were out on their own, living elsewhere.

I hadn't lived alone since 1992, and it frightened me. I put bells on the front and back doors and kept a can of wasp spray by my bed in case anyone broke in. My bedroom was very small, crammed with a bureau, a single bed, and a portable clothes rack. One night I was awoken from a sound sleep by a strange noise. My heart started to race as I slowly opened my eyes to look toward the sound. It was dark and I could see a shadow moving closer. Suddenly the shadow was on top of me. I screamed and struggled to get away, finally jumping out of bed. It took a few moments for me to process what was happening. The clothes rack that was next to my bed had slowly collapsed on top of me. After realizing my attacker was a bunch of clothing on hangers, I took several deep breaths, had a good laugh, and went to sleep on the couch.

Breaking up our family while my youngest son was still in high school, working through my childhood pain, writing a book, and living in the seclusion of the pandemic created an incredible amount of guilt, anxiety, and sadness inside me.

Each night, in my tiny, 800-square-foot apartment, I'd sit on the living room floor sifting through stacks of moving boxes filled with marital archives. While I worked on dividing our assets, the totality of my broken family was reduced to piles judged "important" and "not important." Financial statements were mixed with greeting cards full of love from Harvey and school art projects from the boys. I would sob, my tears smudging the ink on another one of my failures.

Music helped me cope. I connected with the desperation I heard in Demi Lovato's "Anyone," clung to my sanity through Barry Manilow's "All the Time," which became my anthem, and shared hope for the world in England Dan and John Ford Coley's "Love Is the Answer."

I was working in the finance department at a school district and still went into the office, but employees had to scatter their schedules and keep their distance. I found a party hat in my moving boxes, bought a chocolate Pepperidge Farm cake, and celebrated my fifty-fifth birthday on a Zoom call with my three sons and my sister Jennifer. The feeling of disconnection saddened me, but eventually I saw that the time away from everyone was a good opportunity to reconnect with myself.

Although the pandemic was devastating in many different ways, it also forced me into an isolation that prevented me from avoiding my feelings. My typical pattern was to fill my schedule and stay busy so that I didn't have to face or feel pain. With the whole world shut down, I spent a whole lot of time with just me. God's timing is interesting. If the pandemic had hit just a couple of months earlier, I might have ridden it out inside my marriage. The pandemic was a very difficult time but was also the beginning of saving the rest of my life.

A few years before I left my marriage, I read *The Dark Side of the Light Chasers* by Debbie Ford and *The Prison Effect* by Alena Chapman. Those books began to open my eyes about the various ways I was keeping myself stuck. During the pandemic, I sought out inspirational help via the internet while I was trying to flesh out my purpose and rediscover exactly who I was. Although I was brought up Lutheran, I was open to any and all spiritual support.

I found comfort each Sunday morning watching Joel Osteen's services on YouTube. I gained spiritual guidance following people like Kyle Cease, Eckhart Tolle, Michael B. Beckwith, and Dr. Wayne W. Dyer, some of whom I had followed before. Their teachings made me think about things differently. Focusing on self-discovery and self-awareness redirected my thoughts from my external circumstances to my internal judgments. I needed a new perspective on being present and allowing all feelings to be felt and processed.

I realized that the only way past my pain was going to be through it. I confronted the origin and subsequent fallout of each word represented on the cover. I returned to my childhood and relived the memories that created my heartache. My resolve was tested often, but I stayed with it, finally allowing myself to *feel* the unfairness and anger. I cried a million tears for the little girl I once was, and comforted myself like I'd wished my parents had done. I reflected on the craziness I had created as an adult by continuing to avoid my internal issues. In other words, I unpacked all my baggage.

Through that process, I realized that I never had time to mourn any of my losses fully. I had lost homes, friends, pets, belongings, schools, relationships, and my innocence. As a child, whenever my parents encountered a problem, we moved to avoid the consequences, and there was never any time or permission to think, feel, or talk about what we were giving up. My nervous system was trained to anticipate what would happen *next*, not to deal with what had already happened.

11

GRIEF

It made sense that as I delved into my past and started to feel the pain in each incident, I also needed to honor the grieving process. I had been stuck in the first and third stages of grief my entire life — denial and bargaining. I moved into the second stage, which is anger, and was quickly heading toward the fourth stage, which is depression.

The grieving process was not new to me, but I always thought of it as something you do when someone dies. Now, I know that grieving is a necessary process for any loss. I needed to mourn the loss of my innocence in a world I had no control over, and the fantasy of how I imagined my childhood *should* have been. Grief doesn't just go away if you ignore it or hide from it; you have to feel your way through all the stages to heal.

The process of working through the phases of my healing included reflecting on painful memories, identifying the belief or unmet expectation that created the pain, allowing myself to feel the pain for as long as it took to release it, seeing the situation through a new lens of understanding, and forgiving myself and others.

During those phases, some conflicting thoughts started to arise. Significant shifts including, *it's not just about me.* Reliving past experiences would change my life, and I was excited about the possibility of overcoming my pain. I wondered how writing about my life and the influences of others on my self-worth and identity would impact my relationships with friends, family, and more importantly, my three sons. *Was I willing to lose any of them?* Fear was back.

Would you love me if you really knew me? started to invade my thoughts. That question implied that *the real me* might not be lovable. My life was the sum of outdated programing, learned behaviors, false beliefs, bad habits, and fear all rolled up into a character I created to protect myself as a child and to hide in as an adult. I was afraid that once I revealed some not-so-nice things about myself, those closest to me would reject me.

Ultimately, I decided I could not be afraid to lose relationships by honoring exactly who I am. The good, the bad, and even the ugly parts all needed to be acknowledged. I no longer felt the need to adapt my behavior to suit others. I had done that long enough. I wanted the freedom of knowing who I am, and being just that.

The more I thought about the pain points of the front cover photo, the more I felt as if something valuable had been stolen from me. The struggle to be safe had overshadowed the chance to organically develop into my authentic self. I was curious how different my protective character was from my true self. I barely remember the hopes and dreams of six-year-old me who thought the world was magical and that I could be anything I wanted, but that was the last time I remember being myself without all the fear.

My protective character had learned at a very early age to be a people pleaser. Putting others first came along with endlessly trying to keep the peace. I was constantly aware of what everyone in my family was doing so that I could predict trouble and minimize the consequences. I feared being disciplined, especially for something I did not do. I thought "being good" would help distract my parents from the problems at hand. I just had to figure out what "being good" meant and then encourage my siblings to do the same. My idea of peace amounted to times when no one was fighting, and no high drama was being acted out.

"The Saint" is what my family calls me, in their out-loud voices, but underneath that, I feel like they are really calling me "The Sucker," or maybe I feel like that myself. I am the only one who keeps in touch with everyone in our family, and I'm always willing to help any of them if I can. I'm also the only one who takes care of Mom. No matter how badly she treats me, I only have one mother. I've poured an abundance of time, energy, and money into trying to make her life better. The parallel of my mom's life and mine proves that changing your outside circumstances alone will not resolve your issues. The difference is that she is still avoiding her demons, and I've chosen to face mine.

I am no saint, but dealing with my mother requires the patience of one. I can't explain the love and devotion I have for her except to describe it as a divine form of compassion.

In thinking about why I do the things I do for her, it occurred to me that deep down I'm afraid of abandonment, especially by my children. Life has a way of giving you back what you put out there, and I'm not sure if I've fully paid for all of my karmic debt.

The final stage of grief is acceptance, and for me this includes not only my childhood disappointments, but how my childhood affected my behavior as an adult. *Was I a bad person for lying, cheating, and sleeping with married men? Was I a bad partner for never being fully committed to any relationship? Was I a bad mother for moving my kids in and out of homes and relationships with their fathers and projecting my insecurities onto them? Was I a bad daughter for not being able to make my mom happy?* All that judgment added to the feeling that I was "not good enough" and was surely a confirmation that I did not deserve anything better.

My conduct in my teens and twenties with regard to who and how I dated was a copy of what I grew up around combined with a craving for the attention I did not get as a child and my lack of respect for men. Was it wrong and unacceptable? Absolutely. Karma came and kicked my ass more than once and taught me some hard lessons about lying, cheating, and inappropriate sex in those early years.

I now acknowledge that I had no positive examples to follow with regard to relationships. I did not see or experience what I would consider healthy marriages as a child, so I had nothing to imitate. Relationships all looked very problematic, and I had no confidence that any relationship I got involved in would be any different. I started each one anticipating an ending. My walls were up emotionally, and I was not letting anyone get too close — not a very good foundation for a lasting partnership.

Motherhood is a blessing. Although I wanted to be the kind of mother I wished I had, I focused more on what I didn't want to happen to my kids out of the fear of damaging them. I wanted to keep my family together and tried to figure out ways to do that. I thought that if my family of origin could stay together through thick and thin, then the family I was trying to create as an adult should be able to do the same. The behaviors that triggered me in my adult family felt very familiar and detrimental. I couldn't decide what would be best for all of us, staying together or being apart, so we did both, several times.

My dream was to create a home where my kids felt safe to be exactly who they are, where they could talk about how they were feeling and what they thought, where they were comforted when the outside world was beating them up, where they felt like they mattered, where they could find peace, and where they wanted to spend time with friends and family. All the things I didn't have. I felt like I failed them by not modeling healthy relationships and by not giving them everything they deserved.

My mom is disabled and stuck in a nursing home where she feels like a prisoner. I can only imagine how frustrating it is for a woman as smart and as strong-willed as she is to be in a situation where she cannot physically take care of herself. The seed of obligation was planted very early by Mom. To this day she still thinks her kids owe her more attention, a place to live, a better life, and probably even an apology. She continues to blame me for putting her in that home. I can't take care of her so I can't take her out.

By all accounts, the answer to my judgmental questions is yes. At times I behaved like a bad person, a bad partner, a bad mother, and a bad daughter. I'm not trying to make excuses. I'm saying I understand now why I did the things I did and why things turned out the way they did. Most importantly, I cannot go back and change anything that I have already done.

I hear many people say things like "once a cheater, always a cheater" and "people never change." So where does redemption fit in? How much remorse and self-loathing are enough before you are allowed to move forward? Who gets to decide how long you have to suffer for your mistakes, bad choices, wrongdoings, and failures?

Unless someone else has walked the exact same path and has experienced the exact same circumstances you have, no one else has the right to determine how much torment is enough. The only person that can decide on your penance is *you*. I've kept myself mentally and emotionally enslaved to condemnation and guilt for more than thirty years. I've judged my own sins and served a longer self-imposed sentence of shame than the sentences most criminals serve in jail. All while working toward some undefined "finish line" so that I could begin to feel worthy of having a better life. *How much is enough?*

The word "enough" is completely subjective. It's an arbitrary measurement that is solely based on each individual person's level of what is acceptable. If there are eight billion people on this planet, there are eight billion opinions or beliefs about how much suffering or penance is enough.

No one will ever be harder on me than I've been on myself. Now that I'm aware that I get to decide how much is enough for me, I'm confident that I've had enough. Judgment, guilt, shame, blame, condemnation, and regret are a large part of the baggage I have now unpacked. It's up to me to put an end to the judgment because a lifetime of regret is too long!

The same can be said about feeling "not good enough." That is another arbitrary measurement we impose on ourselves based on the feedback of others, giving too much value to what others think of us. As a child, I could not understand the complexities of my parents' issues and our circumstances, so I internalized blame and felt unworthy. I now understand that I did not have the maturity to process the experiences I was going through.

God made us all unique. Usually, things that are one of a kind are considered valuable. *Why is it so hard for us to see and believe in our own worth?* We've all done things we shouldn't have done. We easily let others off the hook. Why not extend the same courtesies to ourselves? No one gets to decide your worth except *you.*

Have I felt guilt and regret? Yes. Am I sorry for any pain I have caused? Yes. Have I learned from my mistakes and made better choices? Yes. Do I think people can change? Yes. If you're willing to own your behavior, express regret for any harm done, and do your best not to repeat the offenses, I believe that is *enough* to continue forward with your life.

As I worked my way back and forth between the stages of grief and examined my character and behavior, I began to realize that acceptance leads to forgiveness. I accept that I am human, therefore I am flawed, and I will continue to make mistakes. I believe that God has mercy and grace for all our mistakes. We keep ourselves stuck in an endless cycle of judgment and unnecessary torment. *Why do we do it?*

I am not the same person I was thirty years ago. I am not the same person I was last week. I am a work in progress, just like everyone else. I am actively working on improving my life and being a positive contributor to society.

"Do the best you can until you know better. Then when you know better, do better." This quote is widely attributed to Maya Angelou and is one of my favorites. In my heart and soul, I know I'm out here trying to do my best. *What more can I expect?*

I have arrived at the final stage of grief — acceptance. Redemption and forgiveness are gifts I choose to give to myself, along with unconditional love. I have no control over whether others will forgive me. That is their business.

12

MOVING FORWARD

My new approach with the people in my life, including my parents, is a tactic I call "understand, then decide." I try to objectively understand where others are coming from and why they do what they do as it relates to me. Then I decide whether I want to forgive them and/or stay in any kind of relationship, without obligation. This is my life; I get to decide.

I read somewhere that repeating trauma is an unconscious attempt to get it right. I've heard many stories about how my parents were raised, and their childhoods appeared to be very similar to mine. Back then, no one spoke to them about how they felt or what they wanted. They were expected to stay out of trouble and help their families at an early age. There wasn't much encouragement that their lives could be any better than what they were born into.

My parents learned to hide their feelings because their parents hid their feelings, and they shut us down and taught us to hide our feelings as well. We're all a bunch of ticking time bombs full of unexpressed emotions that eventually find a way to detonate, causing severe damage such as illness, addictions, abuse, disease, and many other self-destructive behaviors. Expressing our feelings is essential to our well-being, and we should be free to articulate them in a healthy way. If they are not felt or talked about, the battle rages on inside.

Instinctively, my parents wanted better for their children, but habitually, they did what their parents had done, with a few exceptions. I remember Dad saying, "My upbringing was tough, but I turned out okay." I think they were unaware that their lives could be different. Their stories were more about survival than inspired change, and they passed that on.

My mother is rigid with her feelings. I can't remember seeing her cry but once or twice in my lifetime, and I still feel uncomfortable hugging her. She recently discussed her bitterness toward her own parents with my sister Jennifer and me, and how she still cannot forgive them for her traumatic upbringing, even though they've been gone for a very long time. She told us a story about becoming Miss Cinnaminson when she was a teenager. The beauty queen who represented her hometown. When she came down the stairs in her fancy dress to ride in the parade, her mother said, "You must really think you're something — well, you're nothing special, remember that."

Jennifer spoke up: "You've been treating Denise like that her whole life."

My mom gasped in what felt like more of an objection to my sister calling her out then genuine remorse, then she looked at me. "That's right and I'm sorry." Before I could decide whether she was actually being honest or patronizing, she quickly changed the subject back to herself and how her mother had set her up for beatings from her dad.

Once again, Jennifer chimed in, "Isn't that what you did with Debbie, Denise, and Patrick?"

"What was I supposed to do?" Mom's face revealed her developing impatience to our dialogue. None of us were heard during that interaction — proof of how dysfunction gets passed down.

Our conversation sparked memories of shopping for greeting cards for my mother. I would go through almost the entire Mom section before settling on the most generic card I could find. All the other cards said things like, *Thanks for being my best friend, You've been my greatest role model, I can talk to you about anything, Thanks for all of your support.* I felt as if I'd be lying if I got her one of those. Buying cards for Mom made me sad — I wondered what it would be like to feel that way about my mother. I would envy the kids who had moms who were their best friends or biggest supporters. My mom would turn the card over to see how much you paid for it before she read what was inside.

My stepdad, Lou, was the main breadwinner and disciplinarian. When he called your name, he expected you to run to see what he wanted, sometimes jokingly saying, "What would you be doing if I didn't call you right now?" He was very upbeat except for when he was mad. A stereotypical dad who came home from working hard, ate dinner, walked the dog, put out the trash, and sat in his special chair to read the newspaper. He had his nights out with the guys. When he was home, it felt like he was always on edge, especially when my mother pushed his buttons, which she did often.

They planted the seeds of doubt in me like their parents did in them and convinced me that "life is a struggle." That belief was repeated so often that it got buried deep inside and became part of my DNA. I subconsciously lived my life by this belief, proving it was true. It's how I've talked to myself and commiserated with others. *How then can I possibly expect a different outcome or things to be easier?*

Now, I choose to believe life is an adventure. With the acceptance of all its peaks and pitfalls and without the limiting belief that our existence means struggle, life becomes its own form of beauty. I'm no longer fighting against my embedded history, but open to what each day offers me. If something doesn't feel right or fit right, I let it go to make room for what feels amazing.

For all the years I judged my parents and thought they should've done better, I didn't understand that they just didn't know any better. "I did the best I could," Mom always said. I hated that expression; it sounded like a cop-out. *No one could be doing their best and mess it up that badly.* I didn't understand that she was operating from the programmed beliefs of outdated generations combined with a bitterness and resentment toward her own parents.

Now, as I trace my own history, especially as a mother, I know I've tried to do the best I could and have still fallen short many, many times.

Mom made me feel like I was not good enough, but she too, was not good enough for me. Judgment was there in every interaction we've had, reflecting back at her, which kept her in a state of reaction and defensiveness. I may not have spoken the same words of criticism, but I'm sure she felt it. Her disapproval of me taught me how to disapprove of her — another example of how dysfunction gets passed down.

Through my healing process I have gained a better understanding of why my parents are who they are, and more aspects of my childhood make sense. I'm not saying that anything they did to hurt me is okay. I'm saying I have found compassion for their struggles and forgiveness for them. I decided to continue my relationship with them and to love them unconditionally. Only when you have respect, acceptance, grace, forgiveness, and love for yourself can you offer it to others.

I believe God blessed me with three sons so that I could heal the dysfunctional mistrust I had with men. In raising them, I was able to observe how boys feel, think, and act from day one. Because my sons are all very different, I got to see and experience the many challenges and expectations the world puts on boys and young men trying to figure out who they are and where they fit in. I saw that they have feelings, disappointments, creativity, struggles, dreams, and pain, just like me.

I've learned that men are not all bad, as I was led to believe. I do not pretend to understand everything about men now, but I understand that, generationally, men have not been given much permission to talk about or feel their feelings. The emotion I've seen most often in men is anger, which goes back to what I said earlier about repressed feelings being like a ticking time bomb inside of us. Hopefully, that pattern will change in our society.

The thought of another romantic relationship scared me. I did not want to get hurt or hurt another person. In past relationships I chose men who were very much like my mother — I felt criticized and belittled. Now that I have reconciled my relationship with her and found my self-respect, those relationships are behind me. *There is no more time to waste trying to figure out how to make something work that is not working.*

Sharing one's life with someone else is a choice, not a necessity. I knew I wanted to find a long-term relationship. I believed the perfect fit was out there somewhere, and I knew clearly what I wanted. Mutual respect, kindness, and acceptance of each other as we are, combined with the safety of expressing ourselves in all ways, would be a good start. The relationship would have to be a win-win, with equal parts of giving and receiving love.

By the end of 2020 I was ready to start dating again. It had been almost twenty years since I went on a first date. This time around, I knew exactly what I was looking for and what I was not going to accept. I was consciously trying to avoid repeating old relationship patterns and was looking for someone who was also trying to "do it differently" than they had before. I had worked too hard to resolve my problems.

I wanted to open my heart and give a relationship my all, but fully trusting another person would be challenging. Trust was not something I had a whole lot of experience with, but I was willing to feel the fear and do it anyway. Knowing who I am and what I have to offer gave me the confidence to hold out for the kind of partner I deserve.

The pandemic threw a different dynamic into how I connected with people. It was bizarre, meeting and dating on Zoom, or in a mask outside in a park somewhere. I'm not sure if I was more worried about the other person liking me or about getting sick.

Dates are stressful enough, but in 2020, they could be life threatening. It was strange while it lasted, not that dating got much easier post-pandemic.

The online dating sites were not for the faint of heart and tested my newfound self-confidence. Some people are out there thinking they can do better than you without even getting to know you. Rejection is rampant, and I quickly grew a thicker skin to it. I understood that some rejection is not about incompatibility as much as it is about people's unrealistic expectations.

I was genuinely trying to find one special connection but didn't have the available time some men expected I should have for them. I also found that some men didn't like independent women. I was happy with myself, and my life was full of friends, family, and adventures. I felt I could have a meaningful relationship, without giving up myself and my interests.

I really wasn't looking to date casually in my fifties, but dating started to feel like an "all or nothing" choice. I met men who wanted to keep things casual and see several women at a time and men who expected me to give up everything else in my life to solely focus on them. There didn't seem to be many choices in between. I got frustrated and took a break from trying to find "the one." Instead, I started looking for companionship, someone to hang out with occasionally. No pressure and no expectations.

That's when I met Wade. His schedule was as busy as mine, and we were both determined to keep our identities. It made sense that something casual would accommodate both our lifestyles. The attraction was electric! He's tall, with thick salt and pepper hair and beautiful ice-blue eyes that accent the prominent features of his face. He has a strong build and a laid-back hippie vibe. Our compatibility was solid from the start, and we quickly decided to date each other exclusively. The quality of the relationship was unexpected and developed into something extraordinary. Although it was scary, we found a way to progress and grow together with mutual respect for who we are as individuals.

As of this writing, we have been together for a year and a half, and our relationship is stronger than ever. Whether we are enjoying a quiet and casual Friday night with him playing his guitar and singing me songs, or exploring new adventures in places we've never been, there is an ease of being ourselves with each other that makes time fly by effortlessly.

The safety of being vulnerable with our true, innermost thoughts and emotions is unlike anything I've experienced before. Wade's openness has freed me to express ways of being myself that I had hidden in the past. His big heart is full of acceptance for all the layers that make up who I am. I offer him the same in return.

Our families and friends share in our happiness and excitement. We each have three adult sons and hope to get them together for some fun in the future.

∞

They say, "Everything happens for a reason." I believe that "Everything happens for a lesson." My healing process started with a nationally televised court case and an inspired picture of my pain, which led me toward inner peace and self-acceptance.

The journey has not been easy, but it was definitely worth the effort. I've found the answers to my original three questions: *Who am I? What do I want? What do I do next?*

The *real me* is similar to my protective character in that I care about my family, friends, relationships, humanity, and how I show up in this world. I've built healthy boundaries and let go of the need to people please. I no longer need anyone else's approval to feel good about myself — I am self-approved. I've learned to say no to the things I don't want. I no longer make decisions based on fear, but on possibilities. I take 100% responsibility for my decisions, which is the only thing I have control over. I release responsibility for anyone else's life, they can take care of themselves, including my mother who is in a safe environment with her caregivers. I found self-love and know now that I am enough, and I always have been.

I want to continue the new life I've created through my healing process, full of love, joy, freedom, and peace. Grateful for all the blessings God has given me. Sharing my life and all its ups and downs with Wade, the love of my life, and our families. Helping others in need, when I can. Finally, putting generational dysfunction to rest in my family line.

I'm open to whatever life has for me and I've learned that everything I've been through or will go through is part of the journey. I am allowed to be who I am, allowed to feel the way I do, and allowed to want what I want and to go get it!

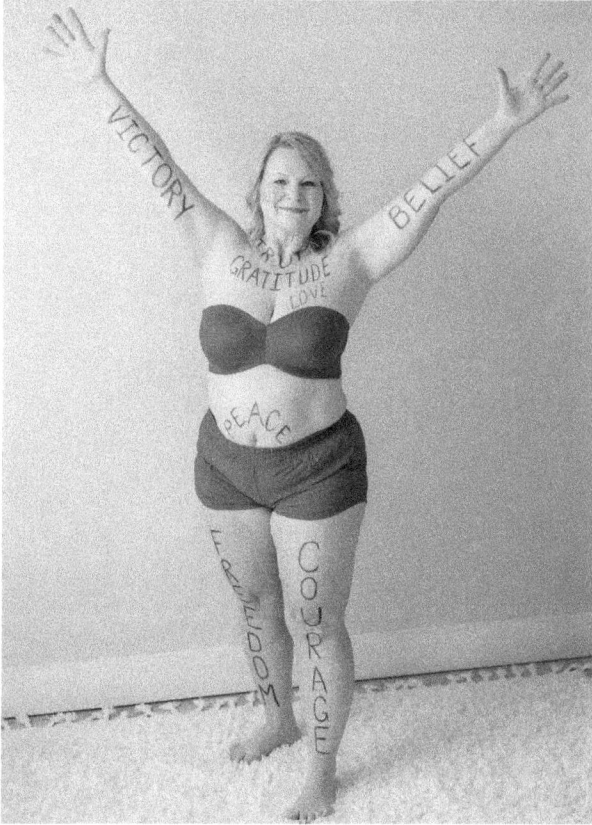

PART FIVE
LIBERATION AND PEACE

No drop of precious love is ever wasted.

—Maharishi Mahesh Yogi

13

LEAD WITH LOVE

The woman represented on the front cover and the women captured in every photo included in this book are all versions of who I am inside. I am my past, present, and future. I am everything I've done wrong and everything I've done right. The difference now is that I no longer see myself as damaged and in need of fixing. I no longer judge myself or beat myself up for making mistakes and being human. I AM FREE!

What I thought was impossible turned out to be within reach all along. Everything I was looking for was already inside me underneath all the BS the world piles on top of us throughout our lives.

I've found unconditional *love* for myself and can extend love to others in a healthier way without expectations or any need to control. *Joy* fills my spirit with a lighthearted state of ease. I am grateful for all of my experiences. I've gained *freedom* from pain, judgment, lack, limiting beliefs, destructive patterns, and the need for anyone else's approval or acceptance. I now allow myself to feel all my feelings, knowing they are here to guide me. They are signals to pay attention to, necessary for healing. I get to choose what is right for me at all times. I embrace *peace* in my mind and body. An almost indescribable level of calmness, creating an unshakable knowing that all is well, and I can handle whatever comes my way.

"Lead with love" are the words I say to myself now in times of internal or external struggle. That mantra puts me right back into my heart when my thoughts start leading me in a painful direction. From my heart, I can bring kindness and understanding to myself and others in whatever situation I am facing.

Those words are invaluable when I reflect on my childhood. I can get to a place of gratitude for all the goodness that existed in my past, and I have an incredible amount of love for my family.

My mother is a force to be reckoned with. She is one of the strongest and smartest women I know. She taught me that God is always with me and will get me through anything. She has helped others when she could barely help herself. I watched her work her way up the corporate ladder to a high-level position in the male-dominated banking world with an eleventh-grade education. I've seen her firmly manage employees with respect and compassion that resulted in the admiration and success of her teams. Her tenacity kept our family together through the most challenging times. Mom's sense of humor and perfect comedic timing is enviable, although I haven't heard her laugh in quite a while. She also has an uncanny ability to make an amazing sandwich out of whatever ingredients are in the fridge that cannot be matched.

Although I felt weak and cowardly around her most of the time, she modeled the kind of strength and determination I relied on to try new things in my own life that were out of my comfort zone. I can find value in everything I did to gain her approval and in the lessons I learned by doing so. Even though the motivation may have come from a place of negativity, the experiences helped me grow into a fiercely independent woman, and I no longer feel weak or cowardly. I learned a lot about resilience and resourcefulness from her and Dad.

My relationship with my mother has been one of the most challenging aspects of my life. I believe now that she loves me and our family in her own way; she just doesn't love herself. It's hard to give away what you don't have. Much of her life has been a disappointment, and she holds on to a lot of blame and anger. The effort and energy I put into mirroring her accomplishments backfired on me. My actions reminded her both of happier times and of the disappointment she carries. Chasing her love and approval pushed her further away because of her own disapproval of herself.

Our relationship is much easier now. I found my boundaries and learned (for the most part) not to be triggered when she is just being who she is, who she's always been. She can't hurt me anymore. I can redirect her judgment, and I've helped her to feel safe enough to revisit her childhood and some of the pain she continues to hold on to. I wish that she could find peace.

My dad (stepdad Lou) was a dreamer — he was all about possibilities. While Mom was bursting balloons, he was filling them up and letting them fly. He worked hard and expected us to do the same. Although he didn't openly talk much about his time in the Navy, he taught us to be proud of the United States of America. He did not talk much about personal things, but lectured us kids with the work-hard speech, the nobody-cares-about-your-problems speech, the be-responsible-and-do -the-right-thing speech, and the family-is-all-you-got speech, over and over again. I used to joke around with him that he could just record those four lectures on a tape recorder and save himself the energy. Dad had a sense of humor and loved to tell long-drawn-out stories with a punchline that cracked himself up. His laugh was infectious. When he and his brother Dave got together, the stories and the banter between the two of them were highly entertaining.

As I got older, I became his confidant. He would talk to me about his childhood, the Navy, relationships, and other personal things. He shared a very vulnerable side of himself. I respected the fact that those talks were not easy for him; I also felt the burden of his pain. I gave him all the credit for keeping me sane throughout our years of chaos.

My sister Jennifer, my brother-in-law Jerry, and I had lunch with Dad a week or so before he went in to have what he described as routine heart surgery. He came out of the surgery well, and we got to talk to him on the phone for a few minutes. His voice sounded scratchy, but he seemed in good spirits. That was the last time I would hear his voice. He experienced complications and was put on a ventilator. When we visited, he was mostly sedated because of all the tubes and machines, but when he was a little more alert, we could talk to him, and he could blink his eyes once for a yes or twice for no.

Everyone, including his doctors, hoped he was strong enough to survive the complications. As the weeks went on, it started to become clear that all those machines were not helping him heal, but they were keeping him alive. It was hard to see Dad in such a weak state. We would put on our brave faces and be upbeat when we went to visit. We hung pictures of the family around his room, and Jennifer brought a speaker to play his favorite country music.

In spite of all of the efforts to make him better, Dad continued to decline. Then came the day we knew that he probably was not going to survive. Jennifer and I stood at his bedside, holding his hands as the reality of what was happening hung in the air between the three of us. I'm sure he could see the sadness in our eyes. For all the years I looked into his soft brown eyes for strength, comfort, advice, love, laughter, and approval, this was the first time I saw defeat. He looked at us as if he was letting us down, unable to protect us from the truth of the inevitable. He asked to be taken off the machines in the middle of the night. We understood he wouldn't have wanted us to see him take his final breath.

Jennifer, Jerry, and I made it there about thirty minutes after he was gone. Jennifer and I got to see him without all the tubes and the machines, and we were able to say our goodbyes. When Lou died, I lost my dad, and I lost myself for a while too. I literally felt like I checked out of life. I lost one of the most important people in my life and a piece of my heart. I think about him every day.

My sister Jennifer has his soft brown eyes. I get to see him every time I look at her. I've saved some of his voicemail messages on my cell phone, so I still get to hear him wish me a happy birthday. I have videos of his infectious laugh from a party where he and my son Steve were breathing in helium from a balloon. Lou was buried in a military cemetery that resembles Arlington, and sometimes when we visit him, we take him a cold Miller Lite, and we have some drinks while we sit and reflect on our favorite memories.

When we were kids, I wanted to be more like my sister Debbie. She was tougher than me, defiant, and gutsy. She was the one who held my hand when we walked to church trying to find a safe place, always protecting me. I was envious of her artistic talents. She sang, played the clarinet, and could draw and paint beautiful pictures. The two of us shared a relationship with our Grandmom Stajkowski and enjoyed being together as sisters, away from the family.

She lives in an apartment in Philadelphia with her husband Bryan and spends most of her time involved with her church. I don't see her often, but we talk a few times a month. I've never doubted her love for me or mine for her.

In 2024, our biological father, Dennis Stajkowski, passed away. Debbie and I traveled back to Florida for his funeral around Christmas. We had gone down there to see him in May of 2024 because his health was failing. We stayed with his family and got to reminisce about his life. Debbie and I talked about our lives and how we wished some things could've been different in our relationships with Dennis. I received closure around who and why I am the way I am. I got to see that Debbie and I were loved by our dad, and he too had wished things could've been different. It turns out I am a lot like him. I've found the missing puzzle pieces I've been looking for to complete my story.

My brother Patrick was such a little wise guy as a kid, always entertaining with practical jokes and impersonations. We'd play for hours, climbing trees, riding bikes, pretending we were superheroes, building secret forts, and making up dance routines. I always felt he was the most like me. We were both on the more sensitive side and covered that up with humor and by staying busy.

He lives in Pennsylvania with his wife Michelle and works as a maintenance manager in a high-end retirement home. Still funny and charming. I don't see him often either, but we are able to pick right back up where we left off as if no time has passed when we do get together. He is one of the only men I have ever felt safe around, and I am very grateful he is my brother.

Jennifer, like my mother, is a force to be reckoned with. She has a hard shell and a fierce protective disposition when it comes to the people she loves. Her determination to succeed is endless. Because she was so much younger than Debbie, Patrick, and me, her early years were not like ours, and sometimes we were jealous of what we saw as her easier life. Then, we all moved out and left her alone to deal with the turmoil in my parents' fading marriage. As a teenager, she took care of our dying great-grandmother before and after school, and she had a front-row seat to our parents' final split. She became the adult, taking care of a mother who suffered deep depression and suicide attempts. Jennifer was repaid by being pressured to choose a side, Mom or Dad, consequently getting thrown out by Mom for refusing to turn her back on Dad. She went through as much hardship and pain as we did, just at a different time.

She lives in Pennsylvania with her husband Jerry and is an executive assistant at a large pharmaceutical company. I admire her thirty-year marriage and that she's been able to keep her family together. They have adopted me into their family functions and we spend a lot of time together. I am very proud of the strong, hardworking, successful woman Jennifer is, and her friendship means the world to me.

My family of origin and the struggles we went through together are a big part of who I am. The hard times made the good times better. There were company picnics, days at the lake, putting on plays, shore trips, happy holidays, and visiting family. I cherish the memories of those fleeting but happier times. We stuck together and found a way to survive. We took turns living with each other as young adults trying to figure things out — counting on each other. Our relationships are far from perfect, but they all have their own special place in my heart.

My three sons are my absolute dream come true. I always knew I'd be a mom. Motherhood has been the best and most challenging thing I've ever done. My wish for Gary, Steve, and Christopher is that they take the time to find out who they really are and be just that, without feeling like they need to please anyone else, and I can see that they are working on that. I hope they don't wait as long as I did to love themselves and forgive themselves for any self-judgment. That they take their lives back from anything or anyone who is holding them back.

I brought my fears from my childhood traumas into my parenting and projected them onto the boys, raising them based on my wounds and disappointments. Treating them as if they had developed the same coping skills as I had. Trying to fix the damages of my upbringing through trying to control theirs instead of recognizing the differences. Unnecessarily protecting them from experiences I perceived to be threatening through the eyes of my insecurities. I wished I had asked them more about how they were feeling instead of assuming I knew.

Our relationships are free to be whatever we want them to be, not based on any societal expectations or beliefs about what a parent-child relationship should look like. I love them unconditionally and that is the only thing I can control. It is up to each of them to decide what kind of ongoing relationship they want to have with me. They do not "owe" me anything.

Gary is thirty-one, Steve is twenty-seven, and Chris is twenty-one. I am grateful to have a loving relationship with each of them. They are free to ask or discuss anything they would like with me, even if it's difficult. I am very proud of each of them and the kind and caring young men they've become in a world that is sometimes not so kind. I will always be here to support them.

Author's Note: In April 2025, just prior to this book's publication, my mother passed away suddenly. My enduring love for her will strengthen me as I navigate this new chapter of my life without her.

14

IT'S NEVER TOO LATE TO LOVE YOUR LIFE

In Wade, I've found a partner who genuinely wants to know me and all my layers. I want to know the same about him. I feel safe to completely be myself and free to talk about anything without judgment — even the woo-woo, hippie-dippie stuff. He is open, honest, and very respectful. A really good guy who is fun and funny. I have opened my heart and trust the love I have for him and get from him. The deep connection I hoped for has become a reality — I have both feet in now, fully committed to our journey. There are no guarantees in life and we both know that. We've discussed our future and chosen to hop on the roller coaster together. We'll see what happens as we share every new version of ourselves.

I am the happiest I've ever been in my life, in a place I never thought was possible — comfortable in my own skin. I am solid in who I am and know that I am loved. Faith, grace, hope, gratitude, acceptance, and forgiveness are all inside me. I have them and I can share them with others. I can count on them to strengthen me in the times when some of my human choices are not so good.

Life is what you think it is. For a long time, it was chaos, instability, dysfunction, and struggle. Now, my days are filled with love, joy, freedom, and peace. The healing journey changed my beliefs and taught me many things.

When I catch myself jumping to conclusions or feeling defensive, I don't get caught up in ruminating about the situation. I question my beliefs surrounding the circumstances and reflect on where they came from. *Is it something my parents or extended family taught me? Is it a false belief or outdated programming? Is it a societal ideology? Is it true?*

This is my life; I get to do with it what I want. That realization was huge. No one else gets to write my story for me anymore, and I make no apologies for living or doing what I want. I've given myself the key to freedom.

Don't argue with reality. I learned this from following Kyle Cease. For many years, I tormented myself over the way I thought my childhood, my parents, and my relationships "should" have been. My past is what it is; disapproval won't change it. Instead of self-imposed suffering over unmet expectations, I try to understand and accept exactly what is.

For sanity's sake, I had to learn how to create healthy boundaries with others. There are a lot of takers in the world. Learning to recognize who they are and how to say "no," has limited their drain on my energy and helps me keep my peace.

If I can't overcome the fear, I have learned to be afraid and do it anyway, and writing this book has certainly produced some fear. My comfort zone has become a temporary stop instead of a full-time residence.

I am not just here to feel good, I'm here to feel everything. All emotions are normal and necessary. During the writing of this book and my healing journey, I've felt a lot of different emotions rise up: shame, anger, love, sadness, appreciation, fear, hope, judgment, gratitude, resentment, empathy, and regret. Some of them were very unpleasant, but I let them fully run their course. A validated feeling has less power over me. In the past, I've either shut them down or distracted myself, usually with something that was not good for me. The results of sitting still, breathing deeply, and feeling the feelings are far superior.

It's never too late to follow my dreams and change my life. Some people get stuck thinking, "It's too late." Realistically, it is too late for me to become a professional figure skater, but for most of the manageable dreams we dare to reach for, it's never too late. When I think of a goal or something I want to change in my life, I ask myself one question: "What's the worst thing that could happen if I do this?" Most of the time, the answer is something I can handle. Then I feel the fear and do it anyway!

It's okay to talk about all of it. The title, "Let's Talk About It," was inspired by the fact that my family hardly talked about anything. We went through everything you've read in this book and so much more but never talked about any of it. I believe that if my parents had been more transparent about our circumstances and my siblings and I had talked more amongst ourselves about our fears, my story may have been different. If we had talked to our parents about the babysitter's behavior, maybe we wouldn't have stayed so long, and maybe Tommy and Becky would have found a new home. If I had talked about the sexual abuse, perhaps I could have saved another child from going through the same thing. If I had talked about how overwhelmed I was as a single mom, maybe I could've gotten help. If I had talked about what I needed in my relationships, maybe I would've gotten what I needed, and they wouldn't have ended. If I had talked about my anxiety, maybe I wouldn't have missed out on experiences that overwhelmed me. I can only move forward, having learned my lessons. Now, I have the skills to create the life I am worthy of living ... the life I've dreamed of.

ACKNOWLEDGMENTS

First, last, and always — thanks be to God for walking alongside me through this journey.

Special thanks to my family of origin, the family I grew up in. I have so much love and gratitude for my siblings: my older sister, Debbie Skoczalek, who always tried to protect me; my younger brother, Patrick McLeester, who always put a smile on my face; and my baby sister, Jennifer Magallanes, who always had my back. You were the only consistent part of my childhood and my very first friends. Thank you for your love and support.

Thank you to my mom, Patricia Blau, for all your contributions to the development of who I am. It's been quite the ride. I love you.

In memory of my stepdad, Lou McConnell, who kept me sane and encouraged me to fly, your love, optimism, and vision helped me to see that the world is full of possibilities, and that we all need to help out where we can. I miss you every day.

In memory of my birth father, Dennis Stajkowski, although our time together was brief, I cherish your kindness and acceptance. Thank you for loving me.

Gary Geers Jr., Stephen Geers, and Christopher Ernst, you are the greatest blessings of my life, and it has been my privilege to be your mom. Your love fuels my belief in everything good and magical about life. You helped me to see what true unconditional love is — I love you so much!

My stepdad always said, "Family is everything." To everyone else who makes up my interesting and eclectic extended family, you all mean the world to me, and I treasure our relationships and the lessons I've learned from each and every one of you.

To my new love, Wade Greim, thank you for generously giving me the space I needed to accomplish my dream. You've listened with an open heart, held me when the process got hard, gently shared your insights, and accepted me for who I am. You are an amazing man, and I am extremely grateful that we found each other.

I am fortunate to have many friends who have supported me through the writing of this book by sharing, listening, caring, and encouraging me. I am forever grateful. To my closest friends Margie Sauer, Mae Gordon, and Jeff Collins, who have listened to me work out my issues and held my hand through all kinds of changes, thank you for being the special kind of people I can count on. Your friendship, support, and humor throughout the years are deeply appreciated.

To the Book Doulas, Kris and Debra, your Book Incubator Program and Writer's Retreat gave me the foundational tools I needed to move my book project forward and helped me to trust myself as a writer. Our time together was priceless and inspired me to keep going. Thank you both for caring about me and my dream.

To my retreat sisters and fellow authors: Helen Burke, you are an angel on earth — thank you for your endless love and support; Helena Grant, who challenged me to see myself as both the villain and hero of my own story, you were right; and Linda Berthelson, who generously shared her wisdom as a published author, it's been a gift to share our journeys.

Thank you to Megan Williams, Ira Vergani, and the entire "dream team" at TSPA, The Self Publishing Agency, for your guidance, professionalism, patience, and encouragement. Special thanks to my editor, Tara McGuire, who helped pull the intricacies of my story out of me with understanding and compassion. You are a special person. It has been a great pleasure to work with you all. You've helped me bring a lifelong dream to fruition, and I couldn't be more grateful.

To Jessica Terkowski of Jessica Lynn Photography, much gratitude for taking my roughly sketched stick figure drawings and some crayons and creating such vividly charged photos encompassing my deepest emotions, allowing a story to be told in a single picture — twice.

To Sherry Coggins, my first life coach, who helped me navigate the beginnings of my midlife transformation in my early fifties, thank you for being *you*. From the first day we met, I felt a divine connection and deep understanding of the challenges women face as we get older ... and wiser. Your light shines brightly and you helped to pull out the untapped courage that I suspected was inside of me. Our work together was deeply impactful, and I consider you a friend for life.

To Kyle Cease, my spiritual guide and transformational coach, who helped me to see myself, my worth, and my place in this world through a whole new perspective, I am honored to have worked with you personally and to have been a consistent member of your Evolving Out Loud community for the past several years. You opened my eyes to a new way of "being" and the power of "presence in the now" that has changed me forever. I am beyond grateful for you and your amazing team. Thank you!

To Tony Robbins, Jim Rohn, Debbie Ford, Bob Proctor, Dr. Wayne W. Dyer, Oprah, Jack Canfield, Eckhart Tolle, Michael B. Beckwith, Brené Brown, Shefali Tsabary, Iyanla Vanzant, Alena Chapman, Gretchen Rubin, and so many more of the incredible teachers we all have access to in the world of "self-help and transformation," I am eternally grateful for the impact you've had on my life throughout the years.

Lastly, to my new family — my family of readers. Thank you from the bottom of my heart for choosing to spend your precious time getting to know me and my story. I wish you all *love, joy, freedom,* and *peace*!

ABOUT THE AUTHOR

Denise Stajkowski is making her debut as an author with her deeply personal memoir, *Let's Talk About It*, which explores her unique experiences of generational dysfunction handed down through a childhood full of chaos, instability, and constant change. Having navigated the ingrained beliefs of unworthiness and insignificance that held her back from living her best life, she has emerged with a stronger sense of self and a desire to connect with readers through her honest and heartfelt storytelling. A wearer of many hats, she is a devoted mother, entrepreneur, self-help enthusiast, and trauma survivor committed to living a life of joy. Denise resides in the suburbs of Philadelphia, Pennsylvania.